THE RISE AND FALL OF A 'CASINO' MOBSTER

THE TONY SPILOTRO STORY THROUGH A HITMAN'S EYES

FRANK CULLOTTA
DENNIS N. GRIFFIN

WILDBLUE PRESS

WildBluePress.com

Some names and identifying details have been changed to protect the privacy of individuals.

*THE RISE AND FALL OF A 'CASINO' MOBSTER
published by:
WILDBLUE PRESS
P.O. Box 102440
Denver, Colorado 80250*

WILDBLUE PRESS is registered at the U.S. Patent and Trademark Offices.

ISBN 978-1-942266-95-2   Trade Paperback

ISBN 978-1-942266-94-5   eBook

*Interior Formatting/Book Cover Design by Elijah Toten
www.totencreative.com*

WHAT OTHERS ARE SAYING ABOUT
THE RISE AND FALL OF A 'CASINO' MOBSTER

I was assigned to the FBI's Las Vegas field office in August 1980. Upon my arrival I was named co-case agent for the investigation of Tony Spilotro's street crimes, which were being run by Tony's lieutenant, Frank Cullotta, and his Hole in the Wall Gang. Frank was Tony's boyhood friend and knew more about Tony and his criminal activities than anyone else. In 1982 Tony and Frank had a falling out and a contract was issued on Frank's life, resulting in him rolling and becoming a government witness.

In this book Frank reveals his intimate knowledge of Tony Spilotro and what really went on in Las Vegas. It's a story only Frank could tell.

Dennis Arnoldy, FBI (retired)

Frank Cullotta was a close friend of Tony Spilotro and served as his lieutenant in Las Vegas. In *The Rise and Fall Of A 'Casino' Mobster – The Tony Spilotro Story Through A Hitman's Eyes*, Frank sets the record straight about Tony the man and Tony the mobster. It's an eye-opener.

Frank Calabrese, Junior,
author of *Operation Family Secrets*

For many years Frank Cullotta was one of Tony Spilotro's closest friends and criminal associates. He was the technical consultant on my film, *Casino. The Rise and Fall Of A 'Casino' Mobster – The Tony Spilotro Story Through*

A Hitman's Eyes, he provides extraordinary insights into Tony's career and the demise of the Chicago Outfit in Las Vegas.

Nick Pileggi, author and screenwriter

I began working as a cop in the Las Vegas Metropolitan Police Department in 1976. In 1978 I was promoted to detective and assigned to the Criminal Intelligence Bureau. In the early 1980s my squad worked jointly with the FBI to bring down the Chicago Outfit's operations in Sin City. Our primary targets were Tony Spilotro, his street lieutenant Frank Cullotta, and their crew.

In this book, Frank relates the real story of Tony and his reign as Vegas's crime kingpin. It's a narrative that only a man with Frank's inside knowledge could tell.

Louie DeTiberiis, Las Vegas Metropolitan Police Department (retired)

For nearly fifty years I made my living as a "fixer." I fixed horse races. In 1972 I visited a friend who was incarcerated in the federal prison in Terre Haute, Indiana, and he introduced me to another inmate, Frank Cullotta. I was having trouble with my business partner at that time and asked Frank if he could help me out. When he was released Frank introduced me to Tony Spilotro. My problem was resolved, and a relationship developed that was very profitable for all of us.

Frank is the real deal and when it comes to Tony Spilotro, nobody I'm aware of was closer to him than Frank.

CONTENTS

ACKNOWLEDGEMENTS

Although the vast majority of the information contained in this book is from my personal knowledge, public records, and newspaper accounts, I wish to expressly extend my gratitude to two individuals whose cooperation and assistance were invaluable to me.

Former federal prosecutor and retired U.S. Magistrate Judge Lawrence Leavitt provided the background of what was known as the Bertha's trial, in which Tony Spilotro was one of the defendants charged with racketeering.

I also want to acknowledge retired FBI agent Dennis Arnoldy for his contributions and support.

Frank Cullotta

DEDICATION

To my deceased parents, Joseph and Josephine Cullotta; my late sister Jean Cullotta Siers; and my brother, Joseph Cullotta.

FOREWORD

By William Ouseley, FBI (retired)
Author of *Mobsters in Our Midst* and *Open City*

Twenty of my twenty-five years as an FBI agent were spent working organized crime cases out of the Kansas City field office. One of those investigations involved the conspiracy between several organized crime organizations, including those in Kansas City and Chicago, to skim money from the Las Vegas casinos.

Nick Civella headed the Kansas City group for over thirty years. Although he was not as well known to the public as bosses from bigger cities, Civella was highly regarded by those other leaders for his criminal abilities and strong political connections. He also had ties to an individual from an organization that would prove to be critical to organized crime gaining hidden control of several Las Vegas casinos. The wily Civella had cultivated and gained influence over Roy Lee Williams, leader of the local Teamster Union. Williams would become director of the union's Central States Pension Fund, which came to be known as the "Mob's Bank" and supplied the cash for organized crime-controlled casinos to be purchased or built in Vegas. Civella's ability to control Williams made him a critical player in the scheme to loot the casinos.

During the Mob's heyday in Las Vegas, the protocol was to keep a low profile—fly below the radar, as they say. Most of the Mob bosses at the time were old school and held the traditional Mafia values of honor, respect, discipline, and loyalty. But they were a fading breed, and a number of young reckless men—indifferent to tradition and motivated by unchecked ambition, greed, and ego—were coming up through the ranks to replace them. One of those men was Chicago's Tony Spilotro.

In 1971 Spilotro was sent to Las Vegas by his superiors to keep an eye on the Mob's interests there. He was a good choice on one hand because of his well-earned reputation as a ruthless enforcer, who would do whatever it took to eliminate business threats and keep things in Sin City running smoothly.

However, appointing Spilotro to that important position had a downside as well. Once in Vegas and away from his bosses, he treated it as his personal fiefdom, importing a crew of thugs, thieves, arsonists, and killers to set up his own criminal empire. One of his street lieutenants was Frank Cullotta, a man who had been his friend since they were teenagers running wild on the streets of Chicago. Over their decades-long relationship, nobody knew more about Tony's criminal activities than Cullotta.

As time went by and Spilotro's organization grew, rather than operating in the shadows, he and his gang wreaked havoc in Vegas. He became very high-profile and a major target for local and federal law enforcement. He was charged in four separate cases investigated by the FBI. Tony Spilotro's conduct became an embarrassment to his bosses and brought tremendous heat on him and them. In 1986 he paid the ultimate price for it.

AUTHORS' COMMENTARIES

By Denny Griffin

I first spoke with Frank Cullotta by phone in 2005 while doing research for my book *The Battle for Las Vegas*. The following year we met in person in Las Vegas and agreed to co-author Frank's biography, *CULLOTTA*. Although Tony Spilotro, Frank's one-time friend and criminal associate, was frequently mentioned in that book, it was Frank's story. In 2013 Frank and I conspired on another book, *Hole in the Wall Gang*, which also included Tony but was again, Frank's story.

In 2015 Frank asked me if I'd be interested in doing another book with him. He explained that he was getting up in age and wanted to set the record straight about Tony Spilotro—to correct the misinformation about Tony that is out there and provide his personal insights about the man, his rise in the Chicago crime family called the Outfit, his fall from grace, and ultimate murder by his former associates. He said this book would be different in that the focus would be on Tony and not him. It would include his personal knowledge and beliefs about murders that Tony committed, ordered, planned, or was a suspect in. Much of that information would be disclosed for the first time, and several of the murders discussed are still officially unsolved.

I was intrigued but pointed out that several killings had been covered in *CULLOTTA* and *Hole in the Wall Gang*, and I didn't want to just do a rehash of what we'd already written. Frank said that although it would be necessary to talk about some of those killings again because they are part of Tony's history, he assured me that anyone who read the book (including law enforcement) would learn a lot.

In addition to clarifying Tony's role in various killings, Frank said he wanted to discuss the details of Tony's own murder which were revealed in the Family Secrets trial in 2007. During that trial one of the killers took the stand and explained exactly how Tony and his brother Michael were murdered. Frank also said he planned to provide the inside story of Tony's racketeering mistrial in 1986. Finally, the book would contain Frank's opinion on how Tony's poor decisions and ill-advised actions contributed to the Chicago Outfit losing control of Sin City. I told Frank I was in.

During the writing process I learned much about Tony Spilotro's rise from a Mob wannabe to a feared enforcer and boss. I also gained a better understanding of how his weakness for women and his quest for money and power eventually contributed to the Mob's ouster from Las Vegas and in the end cost him his life. I hope you will find reading this book to be as informative as I did writing it.

* * *

By Frank Cullotta

The 1995 movie *Casino* gives a fictionalized account of how organized crime lost its control over Las Vegas. Actors Robert De Niro and Joe Pesci's characters were based on Frank "Lefty" Rosenthal and Tony Spilotro. Lefty was an associate of the Chicago Outfit, and Tony was a made member of the organization. In real life as in the film, the Outfit did rule the Vegas underworld for several years, but their main guys on the scene managed to fuck it up. I know because I was part of it. In this book I'm going to set the record straight about Tony, how he gained power in the Outfit, and how his greed and lack of self-control contributed to the Outfit's demise in Sin City and his own death.

My name is Frank John Cullotta. I was born in Chicago in 1938. When I was around twelve or thirteen I met another kid my age named Tony Spilotro while we were both shining shoes at Grand and Harlem. Tony and I almost got into a fight the first time we met. But later when we realized our fathers were friends, we became friends as well.

From shortly after I met Tony he always wanted to become a "moustache" (made man) in the Chicago crime family, known as the Outfit. He got his wish in the early 1960s after doing several killings, including a couple of guys who had murdered two Outfit-connected brothers and an innocent waitress on Mob turf. After those murders Tony's reputation grew as an enforcer the Outfit could count on to do whatever needed to be done. They rewarded him by making him a member of the organization.

I was a criminal for three decades and worked for and with a lot of gangsters in Chicago and elsewhere, but I was closest to Tony. Over the years we did a lot of crimes together. I killed a guy on Tony's orders and set up two other guys for him to kill. He assigned me to whack Lefty Rosenthal in Las Vegas but never gave the final order.

Before I went to prison in 1968, I introduced Tony to two people in Chicago who became very important to him in his criminal career. One was Richard "Dicky" Gorman. He was a thief and a stone-cold killer who did a lot of hits with infamous hit man Frank Schweihs. I called Dicky a "sleeper" because he committed a lot of crimes and never did any time. The other was Paul "Paulie" Schiro, a thief who became a notorious killer. When Tony met those guys he saw their potential right away. He recruited Dicky away from me and then Paulie. They stole with him, and then he started using them to do hits. Later on when Paul got married, he moved to Scottsdale, Arizona.

Another of Tony's boyhood friends was Joey Hansen. Joey was a tough kid who, like Dicky Gorman, became a guy who killed without hesitation or remorse. In the late 1950s or early '60s, he got in the Outfit's doghouse for causing trouble in Outfit-connected establishments. Boss Joe "Joe Gags" Gagliano told Joey he was sick of him and he had only two choices: "You can either get out of Chicago or die here."

The following day Tony told Joey he should move to California where he had family. Joey took Tony's advice. He relocated and later became Tony's "go-to" guy in California.

In 1971, while I was still serving time in Stateville Prison in Illinois, the bosses sent Tony to Las Vegas to keep an eye on their casino interests there. When I was released in 1974 he asked me to come to Vegas and work with him. I turned him down and stayed in Chicago, but by 1979 there was so much heat on me there that I joined Tony in Vegas and became his underboss. I put together a crew to watch his back and provide muscle for him. For the next few years we ran Sin City.

Having me in Vegas, Paulie in Arizona, and Joey in California to do any heavy work he needed done, we became Tony's core. He'd known all of us for years and trusted us. Anybody who says different doesn't know what they are talking about.

In 1982 Tony and I had a falling out and a contract was placed on my life. Facing the possibility of spending the rest of my life in prison or getting whacked by Tony or some other Outfit guy, I rolled and became a government witness. I testified in court against my former associates, including Tony, and appeared in front of several crime commissions across the country.

In June 1986, just before Tony was going to be retried on racketeering charges in Las Vegas, the Outfit whacked him and his brother Michael in the basement of a house in a Chicago suburb. Their killers were indicted by the feds in 2005 and later convicted.

During the thirty years since Tony's death his life has been the subject of a couple of books, TV documentaries, and a movie—the 1995 hit *Casino*, to which I served as a consultant and appeared in several scenes as a hit man. Some of what has been put out there about Tony is true, some is based on truth, and a lot of it is pure bullshit. Most of the people who claim they knew Tony very well are lying. The only non-relative who knew Tony longer or better than me was the late Joey Hansen.

Nobody alive and free today knows more about Tony's criminal career than I do. Not his widow, adopted son, or brothers—nobody. I was there during much of it, they weren't. And I'm sure that with the exception of his brother Vic, who is deceased, Tony didn't discuss his crimes with his family. He sometimes did with me, though.

I'm almost seventy-eight now, and it's time for me to set the record straight about Tony and what happened in Vegas—to separate fact from fiction and myth from reality. I'll start here and now by clearing up some of the misinformation that is out there.

Let's begin with Tony's highly-publicized nickname, the "Ant." In a book written by the late former FBI agent Bill Roemer, the author claimed the nickname was the result of hearing someone refer to Tony as "Ant" during a wiretapped conversation.

After the press began using that nickname in print I asked Tony about it. He wasn't happy.

"*Nobody* calls me Ant to my face," he said. "I know that one time when I was talking with a friend and we were ready to hang up the guy said, 'Okay, Anth, I'll talk to you later.' Anth is short for Anthony, but these jackoffs don't know the difference."

Roemer also said he challenged Tony to box him and Tony wouldn't do it. No way is that true. The only man I'm aware of that Tony feared was one of my crew, Larry "Lurch" Neumann. He'd have welcomed the chance to duke it out with an FBI agent. Roemer didn't make that claim when Tony was still alive to refute it. He played it safe and waited until Tony was dead.

In another book which also came out long after Tony died, former Chicago cop Fred Pascente claimed he and Tony were good friends. I don't know about the rest of the story, but when it comes to his relationship with Tony, it is all fiction. He may have known Tony, but they never hung out or stole together.

In yet another book, a woman claims her dead husband, a guy named Tom Hanley who was a hit man and was associated with the culinary union in Las Vegas, once had Tony on his knees begging for his life. That's a fucking lie. We controlled that union, and Tony never begged anybody for anything. In the Family Secrets trial, Tony's killers testified that even when Tony knew he was going to die he didn't plead for his life. His only request was that he be given time to say a prayer. The truth is, if Tony was having any trouble with Hanley he'd have killed him himself or had me or my crew do it.

If you read any of those particular books, keep in mind that not everything in them is true when it comes to Tony.

In the pages ahead I'm going to talk about many of my former associates, but the main focus will be on Tony. I'll tell you which murders I know Tony was responsible for—directly or through his orders—because I was personally involved or he admitted them to me. Other killings I'll talk about will be based on information from reliable Outfit-connected sources. And some will be just my opinions. I'll make sure you know which is which.

I'll also correct the record about Tony's personality, his gambling, his womanizing, how violent and tough he really was, and some inside information behind the adoption of his son, Vincent.

When you finish reading this you'll know the real Tony Spilotro and why the Outfit lost Las Vegas.

PART ONE

Chicago

1

A ROCKY START

I'll never forget the first time I met Tony Spilotro. I was just a kid, twelve or thirteen, and I hated school. I was always in trouble with the teachers, and my mother had her hands full trying to get me into a school that could handle me. I loved to fight, too, which caused her even more grief.

Anyway, to hustle up some pocket money I started shining shoes up and down Grand Avenue. One day I noticed a kid about my age shining shoes on the opposite side of the street. He saw me at the same time, and we glared at each other for several seconds.

The other kid hollered to me, "What the fuck are you lookin' at?"

"I'm looking at you. What about it?"

We started walking toward each other, met in the middle of the street, and put down our shine boxes.

He said, "This is my fuckin' territory, and I don't want you on this street. Understand?"

He was short but looked pretty solid, and I figured he could probably take care of himself. That didn't bother me, though, because, like I said, I was a scrapper myself. "I don't see your name on any street signs, and I'm not leaving."

We shoved each other a little bit, but no punches were thrown. Then he said, "I'm coming back here tomorrow, and if I see you, we'll have to fight."

"Then that's what we'll have to do."

I went to that location the next day, but the other kid wasn't there. In fact, it was about a week later when we met again on the street. This time his attitude was different—he wasn't combative. He said, "I've been asking around about you. What's your last name?"

"Cullotta."

"Was your father Joe Cullotta?"

"Yeah. So what?"

"Your father and my father were friends. Your old man helped my old man out of a bad spot one time." He told me his name was Tony Spilotro and his father ran a well-known Italian restaurant on the east side called Patsy's.

I remembered hearing about the incident Tony was talking about. My father (who had been a gangster) liked Patsy and was a regular customer at the restaurant. Back then there was a gang called the Black Hand. It consisted of Sicilian and Italian gangsters who extorted money from their own kind, and my father hated them with a passion. Their method was to shake down business owners by demanding money in return for letting the business stay open. They were making Patsy pay dues every week. When my father heard about it, he and his crew hid in the back room of the restaurant until the Black Handers came in for their payoff. Then they burst out and killed them. After that Patsy wasn't bothered anymore.

From that day Tony and I became friends and started hanging around together. I found out he was a few months older than me, and we had some other things in common besides age and being short. We both hated school and would fight at the drop of a hat.

On weekends I'd see Tony at Riis Park, where he hung out. The first time I went there this guy, who was probably in his twenties, dressed in a shirt and tie and looking like a wiseguy, walked up to me and said, "I'll give you five dollars if you fight my brother."

"Who's your brother?"

He pointed to Tony. "Tony, he's right there."

I laughed. "No, I already had a beef with him. We're friends now."

"Oh, you must be Cullotta. Tony told me about you. I'm Vic Spilotro."

I went over with Tony. A little later Vic came over and

said he'd found a kid for Tony to fight. Tony beat the hell out of the kid, and then Vic paid him the five bucks. Tony said, "Hey, what about me? I did all the work. Don't I get anything?"

Vic laughed. "Not you, you're not getting shit. I'm doing this to toughen you up, not so you can make money."

We messed around for a while longer, and then Tony said, "Come with me, and I'll show you where I live. It's right off Grand Avenue."

On the way to his house Tony told me he had five brothers. Vince was the oldest, followed by Vic and Patrick. And then came Tony and his two younger brothers, Johnny and Michael.

Tony showed me through the house. All the boys slept in one bedroom with three sets of bunk beds. While we were in the bedroom Tony's mother walked in. She was a very tiny lady, and I had the impression she wasn't very happy about me being there. She asked who I was, and I told her. If she knew about my father and the Black Hand thing, it didn't seem to make any difference. I still sensed she didn't like me. She said to Tony, "Hurry up and get out of here, the both of you."

After she left I said to Tony, "I don't think your mother likes me and probably doesn't want me around."

He laughed. "Don't worry about it. She doesn't like any of my friends. If she had her way I'd only hang around with altar boys."

As we walked out of the house Tony's mother and father were in the kitchen. Tony said something to them, but neither of them spoke to me. My name wasn't mentioned, and I don't think the father even looked at me as I passed by. Over time I got to know Tony's parents better. They were hard working, nice people. I never knew either of them to be involved in anything illegal.

After that initial meeting I didn't see much of Tony during the week because of school. But on weekends I'd catch up with him at Riis Park. I saw Vic quite a bit, too, at Riis or on the streets. I became convinced he was a gangster because of the way he dressed and that he always had a big wad of money with him. At the time I didn't really understand what it meant to be a bookie, but I'd see Vic getting slips of paper and money from people. I found out later that he was taking sports bets and his operation was backed by the Outfit. He used to run crap (dice) games, too, in the alleys behind the houses in the neighborhood. Although Tony and I were just kids, sometimes Vic let us in the games. Even then, it was obvious to me that Tony was in his element when he could bet on something.

Another guy I met hanging around with Tony was Joey Hansen. Next to me, he probably came to know Tony as well as anybody. He was jealous of my relationship with Tony, and we had a couple of fights over it. I mention him here because he played a role in some of the incidents I'll tell you about later.

Did I know then what the future held for Tony? No, I didn't. But looking back, it's my opinion that Vic Spilotro was the person most instrumental in Tony taking to the criminal life and becoming an Outfit guy. Tony idolized Vic and his lifestyle. Vic introduced Tony to a lot of his associates as he was growing up—more guys with nice clothes, women, and money. And what may have been even more important: power.

* * *

About a year after first meeting Tony we started spending more time together. The reason for that was we both got placed in the same facility—Montefiore School. It was a place that provided educational services for troublemakers— kids who couldn't get along anywhere else. I was sent there first, and Tony showed up about a week later. I don't think he was into criminal stuff then. But like me, he was a kid that most teachers couldn't control.

The student body of Montefiore was primarily black. (We called them "colored" at that time.) Tony and I were two of the half-dozen or so white kids in the place and were constantly in physical confrontations with the blacks. Another thing we didn't like was having to use public transportation to get to and from the school. We couldn't do much about the blacks, but I figured out how to take care of the other.

I'd already learned how to hotwire my mother's car. I started using that knowledge to steal cars from around my neighborhood. I drove the hot car to school and parked it a couple of blocks away. After school I'd drop Tony off at his father's restaurant, where he worked every day, and then I'd drive it back to my neighborhood. Having our own transportation was nice, but it didn't stop the fighting inside the school.

One day when I came out of wood shop I found Tony in the hallway surrounded by four or five blacks. One of them wanted to fight him alone. "Come on, white boy," he said, "just you and me."

Tony agreed. The black kid picked him up and flung him over his head to the floor. Tony got up and put a beating on the guy. Then one of the other blacks said, "Let's kill that white motherfucker," and they started to attack.

I grabbed one of the long poles with a hook on the end that was used to open and close the upper windows. I swung it at the blacks and caught a couple of them in the head, and then Tony and I ran out of the building.

When Tony told Vic what was going on with the blacks, Vic said it was time we taught them a lesson by going after their leader—a kid named Jackson—and he'd go with us.

A few days later Tony and I didn't go to classes, and Vic drove us to the school in his four-door Mercury. We got there at lunch time when we knew all the students would be in the cafeteria. Vic brought along a .45-caliber pistol.

Vic crashed the car through the gates of the fenced-in

playground and parked it near the cafeteria. Tony took the gun, and he and I ran inside and grabbed Jackson out of his seat at the lunch table. As we dragged him outside to the car he was scared to death, crying, and screaming. The other blacks were shocked. They followed us outside but didn't do anything. We drove away, pistol-whipped Jackson, and then drove back to the school and dumped him off.

Tony said he wasn't going to go back to school. His father didn't want him to and said he needed him at the restaurant. I did go in the next day, and the juvenile officers were waiting for me—they wanted to throw me in jail for the Jackson thing. They wrote me up and told me I couldn't come back to Montefiore. And then they contacted my mother and said we had to appear before a juvenile court judge.

Tony got charged, too, but his lawyer told the judge that Tony worked at his father's restaurant and any action against him would cause a hardship on his family. It worked, and Tony was released to work at the restaurant. I wasn't as lucky and got placed in a reformatory for six months.

After I got out, I got into more trouble and drew nine months in another reformatory called St. Charles. So I didn't see much of Tony again until we were seventeen or so. We would run into one another from time to time and catch up on the latest happenings in the neighborhood. By that time he was making quite a name for himself as a tough guy and a thief. People already respected and feared him.

Just before Tony turned eighteen we talked about the Outfit. I'll never forget his words to me at that time: "Frankie, I'm going to become one of them. Someday I'm going to be a boss, and I'll take you with me."

At that time I didn't want anyone to run my life for me. I said, "I'm not interested in becoming a gangster."

After that we kind of went our separate ways. I was content with being a thief and running my own crew. Tony was pursuing his ambitions of becoming a member of the Outfit, and I heard he was hooked up with some big time gangsters out of Cicero.

And then one day, about a year and a half later, Tony stopped in to see me. He said he and some other guys had a big job coming up with a lot of money to be made. They were short a man, and he offered me the spot. I immediately said I was in. It was then I learned we were going to take down a bank.

2

SOME EARLY SCORES
AND CAPERS

The bank job Tony invited me on was in a small town in Indiana, a couple of hours out of Chicago. There were a total of six guys on the job—me, Tony, my friend Dicky Gorman, two who I didn't know and don't remember their names, and Joey Lombardo, who later became known as "Joey the Clown."

Lombardo was an Outfit guy, and at the time he was known as a thief and juice collector (collecting payments for loan sharks). The word on the street was that he was considered a rising star. That's when I realized Tony was hooking up with the right people for the Outfit career he wanted and would probably go places with them.

We took a scouting trip to Indiana to plan the burglary. Tony, Dicky, and I were in one car, and Lombardo and the other two guys were in another. During the ride Tony explained the job. "You know, these old farmers around here don't trust the banks. They won't deposit their money in the bank, but they will stash it in there in a safety deposit box. A lot of 'em have cash in this particular bank, and the guys in the other car know exactly where the boxes are located. All we have to do is figure the best way to get in and out."

After looking the place over we decided to go through the basement of an empty adjoining building, then up through the floor of the bank, and right into the room containing the safety deposit boxes. We thought it would take us a couple of days to get inside and clean out the boxes so we planned the score for a weekend. It was a lot of time and work because each of the boxes was like an individual safe that had to be opened. But we ended up with over $700,000 in cash plus some jewelry. Tony was nineteen and I soon would be, and we were looking at a payday of around $120,000 each.

Joey Lombardo gave us a dose of reality, though. He said we'd have to pay a tribute to the Outfit. On a score of that size they'd want a lot. Even as young as I was, I knew that's the way business was done in Chicago. If you wanted to operate as an independent thief, you had to pay those guys a street tax if you did something big. As long as you took care of the Outfit like you were supposed to they'd leave you alone. But if you held back on them and got caught you'd get a beating or worse. None of us liked it, not even Tony, but we wanted to stay healthy and be able to do more robberies in the future. Five of us (including Lombardo) agreed and kicked in twenty percent off the top for Joey to give the Outfit. The other guy wouldn't go along and refused to pay his share. That pissed the Outfit bosses off, and they ended up demanding an additional forty percent from everybody. It was either that or they'd take it all. We all paid, including the guy who held out to begin with, and they gave him a good beating besides. It could have been worse, though, because sometimes guys died for less.

When all was said and done, Tony and I each ended up with around fifty grand in cash and got more later when we sold the jewelry we stole. Although it could have been better; it wasn't a bad score for kids our age.

* * *

On another occasion Tony asked me to help him settle a personal matter. He stopped by my house and said, "Frankie, there's a guy trying to give me a fuckin', and I want to teach him a lesson. I figure you, me, and maybe one other guy ought to scoop this bastard up and give him a beating. What do you say?"

"Who is this guy? What did he do?"

"His name is Robin Dragon. He was supposed to arrange to have some legal work done for me. He told me the lawyers wanted three grand, but I found out they were only charging half that. This prick Dragon was planning to pocket the extra $1,500. We'll pick him up, take him to your garage, and work him over."

"Sure, I'll help you out. Who have you got in mind for the third guy?"

"Dicky Gorman, is that okay with you?"

"Let's do it."

Tony contacted Dragon and told him they needed to meet. Tony, Dicky, and I picked Dragon up. I was driving. Dragon got in the car without realizing what was coming. As soon as I pulled away Tony and Dicky went to work on him, tying him up and taping his mouth shut. Then they beat on him during the ride to my place and took him into the garage, where the beating continued.

Tony snarled at Dragon, "You think you're going to rob me, you rotten prick? Who do you think you're fuckin' with, you cocksucker?" He then hit Dragon so hard with his .38 that it bent the trigger guard. Dragon went into convulsions and soiled his pants. When the beating was over, Dragon got down on his knees and thanked Tony for not killing him.

We took him back to his neighborhood and dumped him down a sewer. The following day the newspapers reported that a passerby heard somebody hollering for help from the sewer. The police came and found Dragon all beat up. To his credit, he told them he'd been mugged by unknown assailants.

Tony was well on his way to earning a reputation as a fearsome enforcer—a guy capable of using extreme violence against anyone who crossed him. It was that reputation that brought him to the attention of the Outfit bosses, including Paul "The Waiter" Ricca, and got him a position as an enforcer for an Outfit-connected bookie and loan shark.

Tony was on his way up the Outfit's career ladder.

* * *

After the Indiana bank job I bumped into Tony now and then, but we didn't do any business together for several months. However, I knew he was working as a collector for Sam DeStefano, an Outfit-connected bookie and loan shark. Tony was also making some extra cash by putting his own money out on the street and collecting the "juice" (interest payments). The word was that Sam was happy with Tony's work and the Outfit was impressed with him as well.

Then in early 1959—I don't remember the exact date—Tony called me and said we needed to talk. We set up a time and location to meet. When we got together we shot the breeze about how the money we made from the Indiana bank score was almost gone but we'd had lots of fun while it lasted. Eventually, Tony got around to why he asked for the meet. It convinced me that Tony was indeed an up-and-comer and the Outfit was giving him more responsibility.

"Frankie, there's a job that has to be done, and I can't go on it myself. How'd you like to go to Cuba?"

I was surprised. "Cuba? They're havin' a fuckin' revolution there now. Everybody's killin' each other."

Tony laughed. "No, that's coming to an end; this Castro guy's taking over. But there's still some shooting going on, so you've gotta be careful."

"What the fuck does somebody need to go to Cuba for? That shit ain't none of our business."

Tony's humor was gone. "Yeah, it is, Frankie. The Outfit was running the gambling there under Batista, the guy Castro tossed out. Batista was our friend, and the Outfit was making lots of dough. But Castro is another story. He's shutting everything down, and the Outfit isn't welcome anymore. We've gotta move their money out of there, and I need you to go get it. Take Geno [Geno Chapetta was a friend of mine from my neighborhood] with you. I'll give you the number of the guy you need to contact when you get to Cuba."

Geno and I got into Cuba a few days later, and I called

the guy I was supposed to hook up with. He said, "It's too late. Castro's people cleaned the casinos out. They took all the money, and now they're starting to arrest people. You'd better get the hell out of here while you still can."

When I got back to Chicago I met with Tony. He said he'd already heard about me not being able to get the money and that was okay. That was the end of it.

Thinking about it years later, though, I came to the conclusion they used me for that job because I was young and looking for recognition as a guy who could handle almost anything. By sending me, they probably figured I wouldn't draw as much attention as one of their better-known guys, and because I was being sent into a war zone, if I was killed or tossed into prison it wouldn't be much of a loss to them.

Was Tony thinking that when he gave me the job? I don't think so. Back then we were close friends, and I believe he looked out for me. I'm sure the bosses asked him to find somebody he could trust to handle the Cuba thing, and he picked me. I doubt he thought about or questioned why they didn't send one of their made members to rescue their money.

* * *

A short time after the Cuba deal Tony and I pulled an easy score at a business that gave people advances on their paychecks. Today they are known as payday loan stores, but at that time they were called currency exchange. I came up with the idea of robbing one of them, went to Tony's house driving a stolen car, told him what I wanted to do, and away we went.

The store was closed and had a local alarm on the outside wall. Because Tony and I were both very short, neither of us could reach the alarm. He stood on my shoulders and used a crowbar to pull the alarm down, and we disabled it.

There were two sets of doors. The idea was that a customer would enter through the first set of doors. After they closed and locked, the inner doors opened automatically. We pried the outer doors open. When they closed, the inner doors swung open, giving us complete access to the building. The safe weighed about 500 pounds. We wheeled it outside into an alley behind the building, then brought the car around, loaded it in, and took it to my house. Being young and inexperienced at breaking into safes, we beat on that thing for three hours or so before the steel peeled back. There was only about nine grand in it, but that wasn't bad for a few hours work.

* * *

Later in 1961, Tony contacted me to rob a jewelry store in the Mallers Building on Wabash Avenue. I'm pretty sure his brother Vic turned Tony on to the score because Vic had a lot of contacts who ran jewelry stores in that building. Anyway, Tony said he'd arranged to knock off one of the jewelry stores with some inside help. He didn't want to go along on the robbery, so Dicky Gorman and I said we'd do the job for a percentage of what Tony thought the score would be.

We didn't know it at the time, but Tony's "inside" guys were the two Jewish brothers who owned the store we were going to hold up. They were setting up one of their colleagues who'd be coming in from New York.

The Mallers Building had no security cameras, but if an alarm was triggered anywhere inside, the exit doors would lock, the elevators would shut down, and metal gates would come down from the ceilings to block all the escape routes, making it a high-risk target. If an alarm activated before you could get out, you were pretty much fucked.

The store was on the eighth floor about ten feet from the stairway, and the elevators were operated by attendants. Because of that, we decided we wouldn't take the elevator straight from the lobby to the store's floor. Instead, we'd climb the stairs to the second floor, ride the elevator to the seventh, and take the stairs to the eighth. When the job was finished we'd leave the same way. After the planning was done it was just a matter of waiting for Tony to tell us the victim was in town. Then we'd have to move fast.

When we got the word from Tony, Dicky and I went into action. Wearing suits and topcoats, we drove a work car to the "L" railway station in Forest Park. We left the car in the parking lot, took the L downtown, and checked into the Palmer House, which was located across the street from the Mallers Building. I registered as "Mr. Sterling." About two hours later the phone rang. When I answered, the caller (whose voice I didn't recognize) said, "Mr. Sterling?"

"Yes, this is Mr. Sterling."

"Mr. Sterling, your package has arrived."

Dicky and I left the hotel separately, each carrying a briefcase containing a .45 revolver, and walked over to the Mallers Building. When we got to the store we were buzzed into a lobby area. Dicky flashed a business card that had something to do with private investigations or law enforcement, which got us buzzed into an inner room where there were three men—the two store owners and the New York jeweler. We forced the three to the floor, tied them up, and closed all the blinds.

The safe was empty, but I went through the motions of searching it to make it look good to the New Yorker. Then I searched his attaché case. Inside were packages and packages of diamonds. We had what we wanted, but for the sake of appearances we looked around for another ten minutes.

Dicky left first with the merchandise while I kept an eye on the jewelers. I waited five minutes or a little more to give Dicky enough time to get out of the building and then used the elevator and stairs to get to the ground floor.

I walked across the street to a big department store where the L station was located, bought a ticket, and met Dicky inside the station. We knew the L schedule and that we wouldn't have to wait long.

The train got there about the same time we did. We hopped on and headed for Forest Park. During the ride we could hear the sirens of cop cars going to the Mallers Building. Somebody must have found the jewelers or one of them was able to get untied. It didn't matter, though, because we were safe. We just smiled at each other as the noise of the sirens faded behind us and then were gone.

We got back to our car and went to a nearby motel where Tony was waiting with a guy named Mike who had helped set up the score. We turned over all the stones and then left.

In the papers the next day the stolen diamonds were estimated to be worth a half-million dollars.

When Tony came to my house the next day to give me my cut, he said, "Listen to me, Frankie. Let me set you up with a few accounts on the street where you can loan your money. You'll get back 10 percent a week in juice. Even after you give the Outfit their cut, you'll make out pretty good. Trust me, I wouldn't steer you wrong. I already talked to Dicky, and he's going to do it, too."

Although I wasn't excited about it, I did put six grand out to see how it went. I made some money, but loan sharking wasn't for me, and I got out of the shylock business after about a year.

* * *

My next criminal involvement with Tony came a bit later, after I'd started my own gang and Tony was then working for Outfit guy James "Turk" Torello. Tony stopped by my house and talked to me and my guys.

He said, "Turk's got a thing going that's safer and pays better than the robberies you're doing. We call it the bank route."

"You mean sticking up banks?" I asked.

"No. All we do is lay on [watch] the banks looking for messengers coming in to get money for businesses. These guys follow a routine. If you get behind them in line at the bank, you can tell how much cash they'll be carrying by the color of the bands holding the stacks of money they take out. Once you identify a messenger and know how big a score to expect, you can rob him a week or two later after he leaves the bank."

I was leery of getting involved because it might mean coming under control of the Outfit, but I was intrigued and wanted to hear more. "You're already with a crew. How do me and my guys fit in?"

Tony smiled. "There are enough banks to go around, and I'm an ambitious guy. I can work with Turk and you guys, too. I'll let Turk know what we're doing and kick some money up to him. Everything will be okay."

I wasn't thrilled about having to pay the Mob a tribute. Still, it sounded like easy work with good earning potential and we'd remain independent. I glanced at my crew and got their nods of approval. "Okay, we're in," I said.

A few days later, Tony, one of my crew, and I went to Kenosha, Wisconsin, where we did our first bank-messenger robbery. It was a $20,000 score. The only drawback was the travel; the distance we had to drive to get back to Chicago increased the chances of getting caught. We decided to do future jobs closer to home. For nearly a year we pulled a number of successful bank-messenger robberies in and around Chicago. We made some good money, and Tony took care of the Outfit and kept them off our backs.

My luck ran out when Dicky Gorman and I were watching a messenger in Oak Park to learn his routine for a future robbery. We already knew that when he left the bank he walked across a railroad viaduct, so we parked Dicky's Lincoln near the viaduct and waited for the messenger to come along so we could learn the rest of his routine. We had no intentions of robbing him that day.

The guy showed up right on schedule, but when he saw us he went into a panic. He screamed, "Don't hurt me! Here!

Take it!" Then he threw the moneybag at us and ran.

Dicky and I looked at each other and started laughing. It didn't get any easier than that. We grabbed the money and took off.

As we drove away there were some guys in a car stopped at the end of the alley where we'd been parked. There were wearing blue outfits, and I figured they were probably firemen. We drove by them fast, but not fast enough. One of them got our plate number.

A few days later I got the word that a detective named Tom Durso was asking around for me and Dicky. This Durso worked out of the robbery detail which was under the command of Frank Pape. He was legendary and was credited with killing nine alleged criminals in the line of duty and was responsible for sending 300 more to prison.

Durso was also known as an extremely tough guy. He and an associate, a reputed Outfit enforcer named Mike Gargano, used to shake down drug dealers and thieves, demanding a cut of their scores. The word on the street was that if you failed to pay, you could end up dead. If you were a crook, these were guys you didn't want any part of.

Durso and Gargano grabbed me off the street and took me to the Robbery Detail office at Eleventh and State. Durso, another cop I didn't know, and Pape, beat the shit out of me, hung me out a window by my ankles, and even used a cattle prod on my balls. I denied knowing anything about the Oak Park bank messenger thing, though, and kept my mouth shut through it all. They didn't have enough evidence to charge me, so after the rough stuff they had to let me go.

On my way home I stopped to see Tony, who was then running a restaurant with his brother Vic. He saw my black eye and said, "What the fuck happened to you?"

"Durso and his buddy Gargano picked me up for that Oak Park thing. When they took me to the station, Frank Pape, Durso, and another cop worked me over." I lifted my shirt to show him my bruises.

"What'd you tell them?"

"I didn't tell them shit. If I had, I wouldn't be here now, I'd be locked the fuck up."

"That's good, Frankie. Fuck those assholes."

"You wanna know the worst part? They used cattle prods on me."

Tony seemed shocked and angry. "*What?* Those rotten bastards used cattle prods?"

"Yeah, and now anytime a messenger gets robbed, they'll be looking for me. I've gotta give up the bank route, Tony. I've gotta find something they won't connect me with."

That was the end of the bank route for me, but Tony stayed at it a while longer.

* * *

I want to tell you this story about Tony that I think is kind of funny. In 1961 he married a Milwaukee girl named Nancy Stuart, who was living in Chicago when they met. After the wedding they took a belated honeymoon trip to Europe with another couple. It wasn't just a pleasure trip, though. The main purpose was to steal as much jewelry and stones as possible. The trip didn't go as planned, and when Tony returned, we talked about it.

I said, "I read in the paper that you got locked up over there. What happened?"

Tony laughed. "We were going all over Europe, burglarizing hotel rooms, and getting good stuff. Then Interpol started breathing down our necks. They raided our hotel room, and when they knocked on the door and said who they were, Nancy put all the stones in a jar of face cream. The cops came in, searched, and found nothing. All the while Nancy was holding the jar of cream and they didn't pay any attention to her. They took me in, and questioned me for a few hours, and then let me go."

"So you brought the stones back?"

"I couldn't. The cops were on me, and there was no way I'd be able to get them all past customs at the airport. Nancy put a few of the stones in her hair, and she got them through—they brought me about a hundred grand. But I buried most of the stuff in France. What's there has to be worth a quarter million, at least."

"Buried it?"

"Yeah. I went on a country road and found a tree with a real funny shape that I'd be able to recognize, dug a hole next to it, and buried the bags of stones. When the heat goes off I'll go back over and get them."

When Tony tried to go back he found out he wasn't welcome in Europe. As far as I know he never made it back into France. What happened to those stones is anybody's guess. They might still be buried there, somebody could have found them, or maybe they were bulldozed over to build a shopping mall.

* * *

A friend of Tony's we called Skeets told us he had an "out" (customer) who would buy stolen postage stamps. After hearing that, Tony and I burglarized two post offices. They were both easy scores because post offices didn't have any alarms then, so getting inside was a piece of cake. We took all the stamps that were out in the open and then broke into the safe, peeling the door open using a portable power tool. After the door was peeled we spun the dial, lined up the bolts, opened the door, and took all the stamps.

Postage stamps were five or six cents at that time, and Skeets paid us a penny for each one. That may not sound like much, but we stole hundreds if not thousands of sheets of them, so the money added up nicely.

We quit after the second job because we knew the feds would start setting traps for us and we'd be facing federal charges if we got caught.

Later on, Skeets brought me in on a robbery that Tony wasn't directly involved in. I mention it to illustrate that Tony had risen in the Outfit to a point that he had great power and influence.

Skeets and his crew invited my friend Mikey (a.k.a. Bushelhead) to help them steal a load of Max Factor lipstick from a trucking terminal. He knew that Mikey and I had good work cars, nerve, and experience and could be counted on. He said the estimated value of the lipstick was around $500,000, and we'd probably be able to get $350,000 for it. The tip had come from a dispatcher who worked at the terminal so it was solid.

It was one of the easiest scores we ever did. We brought our own tractor with fictitious plates, hooked it onto the lipstick trailer, and our driver, William Dauber, drove it out.

The trouble started three weeks later when Mikey and I still hadn't received our money. I started bugging Skeets about it. He said the merchandise was in a warehouse and he was just waiting for somebody to come along with the right price.

More time went by and still nothing. I mentioned the score to Tony because he was tight with Skeets. He already knew about it.

"I didn't know you were part of the score, Frankie."

"Yeah, Mikey and I were both there. But this fucking Skeets says he hasn't sold the load yet and we haven't seen our money."

"That's true, he hasn't moved it yet. He's got the stuff stored where it's safe. I'll keep an eye on it and make sure you get the right cut."

Tony not only knew about the score, he knew the load hadn't been sold yet, where it was stored, and would make sure Mikey and I were treated right. You didn't know that kind of stuff or have that kind of clout unless you were a bigshot in the Outfit. There was no doubt that Tony Spilotro was now a force.

This was a situation where even with Tony on my side it was a bust, though. About a week after that conversation Skeets sent the load to Wisconsin to try to get rid of it. The feds busted his driver, impounded the load, and all that money went down the drain. I never got a dime out of it. The interesting thing is that Dauber, who drove the rig to Wisconsin, and his wife were murdered in 1980 and were among the killings charged in the Family Secrets trial that began in 2007. I heard that one of the reasons he was whacked had something to do with that lipstick deal.

3

THE COLONY HOUSE
RESTAURANT

The Colony House Restaurant was located on Grand Avenue at the intersection of Harlem Avenue—one side of Harlem was in Chicago and the other side was in Elmwood Park. In the mid-1960s it was one of our favorite hangouts. There was a Chicago police detective who hung out there, too. He was an arrogant wise-ass, and sometimes he liked to bust balls on the wiseguys.

One night Tony and I were sitting in a booth near the back door, and the cop made a smart remark to us as he passed by. Tony and I were discussing the jerk when Tony's brother Vic came in and joined us.

Vic said, "If he's bothering you, why not steal his car, drive it down the street, and burn it?"

Tony said, "Yeah, why not?"

We told Vic we'd take the car a few blocks away in Elmwood Park and asked him to pick us up there. Then Tony and I walked out the back door and around to the front of the building where the cop's unmarked Ford was parked. I got behind the wheel and jiggled the ignition until the tumblers fell into place and the car started.

I drove to the location in Elmwood Park and pulled over. Tony had brought a newspaper with him from the restaurant, and when we got out of the car, he stuffed it under the seat and lit it. Vic picked us up a block away. We went back to the Colony House, entered through the back door, and returned to our booth.

About twenty minutes later the cop left, but of course he couldn't find his car. He came back inside and made a call on the payphone. He sat back down and gave us the eye, like he wasn't sure what was going on but figured we had something to do with it. A few minutes later he got a call and right after that a tow truck pulled up out in front with the burned-out police car on the back.

The cop went outside, looked at the car, and then came back in. He yelled, "I can't prove it, but I know somebody in here did this or had it done."

Everybody just looked at him.

A pair of uniformed cops showed up and talked with the detective for a couple of minutes. Then they left, and the detective went with them. The cop cars took off followed by the tow truck.

The story made the newspapers the next day, and it was the last time that detective was ever seen in the Colony House.

* * *

Parking wasn't allowed on Grand Avenue in front of the Colony House, but we all parked on the street anyway. Unless you were a cop, you could count on getting a parking ticket most of the time. Whenever I got a ticket I ripped it up and threw it away.

One night a bunch of us were standing on the corner next to the restaurant when a cop car pulled up and the officer started writing me a ticket. I hollered to him, "Hold on, I'll move it."

He said, "Too late," and stuck the ticket on my windshield.

"Fucking asshole," I muttered under my breath.

"What did you say?" the cop asked.

"Nothing."

When the cop pulled away I ripped up the ticket, but he came back around and wrote me another one. He got back into his car, and I ripped up the second ticket. This time I gave him the finger, and he must have seen me in his mirror.

I got into my car, flipped a U-turn and parked across the street in Elmwood Park where the Chicago cops had no jurisdiction. The cop came running over and said, "I'm going to place you under arrest."

I started swearing at him. As I did, a large group of my friends gathered around us. I don't know where they all came from, but they were there. Tony hadn't arrived yet, but his brother Johnny was in the crowd.

We started taunting the cop, knowing we were in Elmwood Park and he didn't have any authority there. The gang surrounded him and actually disarmed him. That's when Tony showed up. He was laughing and said, "You fucking guys are crazy."

I said, "This asshole gave me two tickets and then came over here to arrest me."

About then the chief of police from Elmwood Park pulled up. He calmed things down and told the Chicago cop they'd have to take me into his station and figure out what to do. I got into the chief's car, and the Chicago cop, Tony, and the rest of the guys followed us to the station.

I was sitting in their lockup when one of the cops came in and said, "Man, you've got problems."

"What are you talking about?"

"Your buddies broke all the windows out of the Chicago police car and flattened all the tires."

I laughed. "I had nothing to do with it. I've been locked up in here."

Chicago sent a paddy wagon to Elmwood Park to transport me to one of their precinct stations. As we were driving down the street I saw a car with two guys in it following us. One of them was Tony, and the other was named Jimmy, a burglar from New York.

When I got to the precinct all the cops, including some big brass, started screaming at me for what had happened to their officer and their car. They wanted to charge me with inciting a riot but decided that wouldn't stick. They ended up with a vandalism charge and set bond for me, which Tony (who was a licensed bail bondsman) posted right away.

Tony was pretty tight with an Outfit-connected politician named Pat Marcy and got me an appointment to see him. I also contacted Patty Petrone, who had been a political friend of my father. Pat and Patty arranged for a meeting in the judge's chambers. The cops were really pissed off about the whole thing and ranted and raved. But thanks to Pat and Patty and their clout, I was fined fifty bucks and the case was closed.

* * *

Usually when Tony and I met up at the restaurant we'd go out gambling or drinking, but he had a crazy sense of humor and sometimes we'd pull some nasty tricks on our friends. One of our favorites was to get a guy to take a ride with us and then I'd hold him while Tony cut his hair.

We started getting a bad reputation in the neighborhood, and it got harder to get guys to get in the car with us. But one day this kid named Rudy said he'd go for a ride. Tony already had planned that whoever went with us was going to get stripped naked and put out on the street.

When we got Rudy nude we pushed him out of the car and watched him run down the street. It was funny as hell because other than being naked, he looked like any other jogger. At nineteen or twenty years old, it was one of the funniest things I'd ever seen. We picked him up after a block and let him get dressed.

When the word got out about what we did to Rudy, nobody else would get into our car with us.

4

TONY THE GAMBLER

Tony didn't spend all his time committing crimes or pulling pranks—he also loved to gamble. He'd bet on almost anything, but his favorite pastime was playing cards, especially gin rummy—and he was very good at it. He usually played his opponent head-to-head, but sometimes got into four-handed games with two sets of partners.

Whenever he had a big game coming up he'd invite me to come along. He said I was his good luck charm, and he did usually win when I was with him. When he won big he always offered me a cut, but I never took anything. I was doing lots of good scores at the time so I was always well-heeled and didn't need his money. More importantly, though, I think he liked me around to watch his back.

I'm going to tell you about four specific incidents regarding gin rummy games that have stuck in my mind over the years.

The first time I went to a game with Tony—I think it was in the early '60s—I was in the Colony House when Tony came in. He was dressed in a suit and tie—he always dressed very well at that time—and asked me to take a ride with him. We ended up at a warehouse owned by a guy who ran a company that made cardboard boxes. I don't remember his name, but he was very wealthy.

He and Tony played gin rummy for several hours that night, and Tony came out way ahead. After that they played at least once a month. I don't remember Tony ever losing to the guy, and I'd say he usually won at least ten grand, which was pretty big money at the time.

* * *

Tony also played a lot in taverns and lounges. One night

he was in a four-handed game of gin in the back room of a lounge, and I was out at the bar. I heard cursing and yelling coming from the back room, and then Tony and one of the bystanders watching the game—a huge Irishman—came out into the bar area. They were fighting, and Tony hit the guy in the eyes with about ten punches in rapid succession. That was the way he always did it. He was very fast with his hands and knew that when fighting bigger guys it was important to hit them first. He'd nail them with a barrage of punches before they knew what was happening.

The Irishman went down to his knees, and when he started to get up, I saw Tony reach for the back of his waistband. I knew he was going for his gun, so I ran over and grabbed his hand. "It ain't worth it," I told him.

By the time the guy got back on his feet his eyes were just about swollen shut. He didn't want to fight anymore. Instead he apologized to Tony and said he couldn't believe such a little guy could give him that kind of a beating. That was the end of it. Tony went back to the game, and the Irishman stayed at the bar.

* * *

Another time Tony called and asked me to stop by his house. When I got there he was playing Frank "Lefty" Rosenthal head-to-head. Tony beat him for about $60,000. Lefty said he didn't have the money with him and had to go back to Florida, where he was living, to get it. I gave Lefty a ride to a taxi stand so he could get to the airport. Within two days he was back and paid Tony off.

I should mention here that contrary to what you might have heard, Tony and Lefty weren't friends from childhood—Tony knew him from Chicago but never liked him. Lefty was a great oddsmaker and made a lot of money for the Outfit, though, and because of that Tony had to treat him decent.

We were at a joint in Elmwood Park that was owned by a real nice guy named Tony Lombardo (no relation to the Outfit's Joey Lombardo). It was early afternoon, and Tony and Lombardo started playing gin at the end of the bar. Customers were trickling in, and every few minutes Lombardo had to stop the game to take drink orders. Tony asked me if I'd tend bar so they could play without interruption. I didn't know anything about making fancy drinks, but because everybody was drinking beer, I said okay. I did all right, except that I got into an argument with one of the customers and hit him in the head with a beer bottle.

After about three hours of play Tony had Lombardo hooked for $15,000, and he admitted he didn't have the money. He wanted to make a deal for Tony to take over the bar to settle the debt.

Tony said, "Frankie, do you want to go into the bar business with me?"

"Not really. You saw how I deal with customers who give me a hard time. I don't think I'd be good for business."

Tony turned to Lombardo. "Well, it looks like we want the money instead of your joint."

"I tell you I don't have it," Lombardo said.

Tony thought for a few seconds. "Here's what I'll do. You've got five days to come up with the money. If you don't, then I'll have to take your place."

Lombardo was happy and couldn't thank Tony enough. A few days later he paid Tony what he owed him. Right after that the building burned down. I don't know who torched it, but I suspect Lombardo borrowed the money to pay Tony and repaid that loan when he collected the insurance money on his building.

* * *

In addition to playing cards, Tony bet on sports. Football, baseball, hockey, horse racing, basketball, boxing—it made no difference to him. If there was a competition, Tony would bet on it. In fact, when Tony was still an up-and-comer in Chicago, he was a bookie for a while and eventually ran a crew of four or five guys who took bets for him. He kicked a percentage of his profits up to the Outfit. As for his own betting, Tony wagered through other bookies.

When Tony moved to Vegas he didn't hang out in the Outfit-controlled joints because he didn't want to draw unnecessary attention to them. However, he was able to play cards and place bets in the non-Outfit casinos until he was banned by the state because of his Mob connections. After that he'd send some of his friends to the casinos to make the bets for him. He had three TV sets in his living room so he could watch three different events at the same time.

Unfortunately for Tony, he didn't have the same luck in sports betting as he did playing gin. I think he lost more than he won.

One time he told me he was on a losing streak and borrowed fifty grand from a bookmaker who worked for him named Herb Blitzstein. "What's the matter? Are you busted" I asked.

He laughed. "No. I just want to bet with his money for a while."

When Herb asked for the money Tony told him he didn't have it. I don't know if he ever paid him back.

* * *

Tony didn't believe in making bets with his friends. I learned that the hard way in October of 1980 when Muhammad Ali fought the undefeated Larry Holmes at Caesars Palace. We were in a nightclub that was going to carry the fight on closed circuit TV.

I said, "I think Ali is gonna clean this guy's clock."

"No chance. Ali is going downhill, and Holmes will take him easy."

"Care to put some money on it?"

"No. I don't bet into my friends, and I don't want to take your money. But Holmes will win, I guarantee it."

I challenged him, "If you're that sure, why not put something on it? Say $500?"

"If you want it that bad, it's a bet. Just remember that it was your idea."

Tony was right. Holmes dominated the fight. Afterward he held his hand out looking for the $500. I was a little surprised because we were both doing well financially at the time, and I thought he'd just laugh it off.

"I was just playing with you," I said.

Tony laughed. "I gave you a lot of chances to back out, but you insisted. I took the bet to teach you a lesson about not betting with your friends. If it costs you $500 you're more likely to remember it."

He was right again. I paid him the money the next day and never forgot it.

* * *

Although Tony liked the excitement of risking money on games or events in which the outcomes were at least somewhat uncertain, he wasn't above taking advantage of a sure thing.

In 1972, I was in the federal prison in Terre Haute, Indiana, finishing up a ten-year sentence. I only had two years left to do and as a short-timer with good behavior I was transferred to the prison farm. The rules were relaxed there, and inmates had more freedom. About a year after I moved to the farm a guy out of New York named Charlie—who I'd met in the main prison—was sent to the farm.

Visiting rules were pretty loose, meaning the inmates and their visitors could mingle with each other. Charlie had a good friend—a fellow New Yorker—whose name was Larry Rolla. I knew from Charlie that Larry was a "fixer." He fixed horse races to assure a specific horse would win and then cleaned up betting on races he couldn't lose.

One day when Larry was visiting I walked over and Charlie introduced me. Larry knew I was connected to the Outfit and Tony Spilotro. We hit it off pretty good.

On a later visit Larry asked me if I could help him out. He explained to me that he had a stable of race horses at Monticello Racetrack, where he stayed most of the year. In order to get more action, he and his partner agreed that Larry would stay in Monticello and continue fixing races there, while his partner traveled to the major racetracks around the country where he had connections and fixed races.

For months his partner called every day, and they exchanged information on what and how to bet. Then the calls started to become less frequent. They went from every day to every other day and then to once a week. Larry said that the word on the street was that his partner was making millions and calling him only once a week with the crumbs.

Larry said he needed someone he could trust to travel with his partner and keep him honest. He wanted me to introduce him to Tony so he could discuss a possible business relationship with him. I told him I'd be getting out in about four months and then I'd see what I could do. I gave him my mother's phone number so he'd be able to reach me when I was back in Chicago.

After being released I contacted Tony in Las Vegas and told him about Larry and his scam. Tony was very interested. He wanted to meet Larry and said for both of us to fly to Vegas. I was on parole, and if I got caught leaving Illinois I'd end up right back in prison. The potential for making some big money was too good to turn down, though, so I took the risk and flew to Vegas with Larry.

We went to Tony's home where we met with him and Herbie Blitzstein. Larry laid it all out—the agreement with his partner, the connections he made at major racetracks, who got bribed, how much, how the bets were placed and how the profits would be split. An agreement was made that night. Tony told Larry that Herbie would be his back-up man and provide any muscle necessary and to make sure that his partner calls in on every race that he fixed. The next day I flew back to Chicago.

Although from that point on I had no direct involvement with the operation, for the next several months Tony made sure I received payments for making the connection.

I'll talk more about Tony's gambling in the Las Vegas section.

5

BUSINESSMAN

Tony Spilotro was not a lazy guy—far from it. He was a hustler, always looking for ways to make money. Most of the time he chose to earn through illegal activities. However on occasion he was actually legit, used a legit business as a cover, or appeared to be an employee of a real business, even though it was a no-show job. Here I'm going to talk about his actual legitimate efforts.

Other than working at his father's restaurant, the first real business that I'm aware Tony was involved in was in the mid-1950s. He and his brother Vic were partners in a restaurant called King Burger (where I talked with Tony after my beating by the cops) located on Roosevelt Road in Chicago. Because Tony was only seventeen or eighteen at the time, Vic probably showed as the owner of record.

Because of Vic's established connections to the Outfit and Tony getting more and more noticed by them, a lot of Outfit guys hung around the restaurant. The business was run above board, though, and did pretty well.

His next gig was as a bail bondsman. I laughed when I heard about it because as crooked as Tony was I couldn't imagine him being a bondsman. When I learned he was working for Irwin Weiner, it made more sense, though. Weiner was Mob-connected and was standing alongside Allen Dorfman (who handled obtaining Teamster loans for the Outfit) when Dorfman was gunned down in a Mob hit in January 1983.

It was common practice back then for wiseguys to have a legitimate source of income—at least on paper. I don't know of anyone Tony ever made bail for (other than one time for me), so I think it served more as a front to account for how he made his money.

Tony also had an interest in jewelry, either stealing and

fencing it, or selling it legally. As stated earlier, his brother Vic had a lot of connections in the Mallers Building (where we robbed a jewelry store in 1961) and shared them with Tony. Those contacts led to a number of opportunities for him.

One of them arose when he moved to Las Vegas in 1971. Tony opened a jewelry store in the Circus Circus Hotel and Casino. Because gaming regulations didn't allow people with ties to organized crime to operate businesses in casinos, he used the name Anthony Stuart (his wife's maiden name) Ltd. He got his inventory on consignment from jewelers in the Mallers Building.

Las Vegas was a hot spot for selling jewelry then, and Tony was doing okay until the FBI located him and informed the Nevada authorities. Under pressure, the Circus Circus told him he had to get out. He sold the business at a profit and moved on.

From there he got involved with his brother John (who had also moved to Vegas) in a restaurant called The Food Factory. John actually ran the place. Tony hung around a lot, though, and his presence drew business. I want to make it clear that John was a legit guy, and his business dealings with Tony were above board.

Tony next opened another jewelry store that he called the Gold Rush. It was located on West Sahara, just west of Las Vegas Boulevard. Tony was very conscientious when it came to security, and his store had a front door that was operated by a buzzer located behind the counter, and a private security company regularly swept the building for electronic bugs and monitored the building's alarm system.

Tony ran the Gold Rush for several years, but the FBI was keeping a close eye on him and anyone associated with him. In March 1978, they obtained authorization from the court to use wiretaps and other electronic surveillance methods. By June they had enough probable cause to get search warrants for eighty-three locations suspected of containing evidence of criminal activity, including the Gold Rush. On June 19 the warrants were executed, and the feds pretty much emptied the store.

What they didn't understand was that Tony didn't use the Gold Rush to handle stolen merchandise that could be identified. He may have been a lot of things, but stupid wasn't one of them. He knew the law was on him and the Gold Rush was a target. No way would he make it that easy for them to put him away.

I'll tell you how the hot stuff was handled. I know because we did it the same way after I arrived in Vegas the following year. If we stole an identifiable piece that contained diamonds, the diamonds were immediately removed and put in different settings. Herby Blitzstein then put the gold in a big vat and melted it down.

If we had pieces that had to remain intact to maintain their value or were simply too hot to bring them anywhere near the store, I personally took them directly to our fence in Arizona or to some Arab jewelers in Palm Springs. Once in a while I even took things back to Chicago.

It turned out that all those raids didn't matter much, anyway. A U.S. magistrate later ruled that the agents had gone far beyond the scope authorized in the search warrants and that nearly all the evidence gathered was inadmissible.

This isn't a very long chapter because as far as I know, these are the only legitimate or semi-legitimate businesses Tony was ever involved in.

6

ELEPHANT MAN

I learned that Tony was destined to be a lady's man early on. Most young guys were interested in pursuing the girls, but none more than Tony. The trouble was that when his dick got hard his other head went soft. It was a weakness that got him into trouble over the years.

The women loved Tony. He was charismatic, but his appeal wasn't just his charm and personality. He was hung like a fucking elephant.

I found that out when we both registered for the draft and had to report for physicals. When we stripped down I happened to glance over at Tony.

I said, "Holy shit. I thought that was a fucking elephant trunk hanging down. No wonder the girls are always screaming when you've got them in the back seat."

He chuckled. "I can't help it, Frankie. I'm hung heavy."

I laughed and said, "Be careful with that thing, or the cops will lock you up for possession of a dangerous weapon."

We both were classified as 4-F—unsuitable for military service. Tony was disqualified because he had flat feet, and me because of my poor eyesight.

* * *

One night when we were sixteen or seventeen Tony and I were out cruising in my car when I stopped at a service station on Harlem Avenue to get gas. I noticed another car at the pumps with three people about our age in it—two guys and a girl. I recognized the driver as a kid named Ron, whose father owned several laundromats. When he got out of the car I went over and talked with him.

"Who's the broad?" I asked.

"She's from Elmwood Park. We just nailed her; she's a

good lay."

"Both of you?"

"Yeah, we both did her."

"Stay here. I'll be right back."

I went over to my car and said to Tony, "See the broad in the convertible over there? She lives in Elmwood Park, and those two guys just banged her. Want to give it a shot?"

"Sure. Go tell her we'll give her a ride home."

Ron was back in the car behind the wheel. I said, "Why don't you let Tony and me take the girl off your hands and give her a ride home?"

I saw a scared look on her face. I said to her, "Don't worry, Elmwood Park is right on our way. We'll just drop you off."

She got into the backseat of my car, and Ron and his buddy took off. After I pulled out of the gas station Tony hopped over the seat into the back and started talking with her. When we got into an area without streetlights he told me to pull over. I stopped the car and got out so Tony could make his move.

I was standing near the back of the car when it started shaking as Tony went after her. I could hear her saying that she wasn't that kind of girl and she wanted to go home. A few minutes later Tony called me to get back into the car, and he jumped into the front seat. We took the girl to her house, let her out, and took off.

Tony said, "She told me those guys didn't bang her. They tried, but she's not into that and wouldn't give it up. She said if they told you different, it was a lie. I believe her."

"That bastard," I said.

I was in similar situations with Tony many more times, and this was the only time he struck out.

I bumped into Ron a few weeks later and punched him out for lying to me. I never saw him again.

* * *

Tony spread himself around when it came to stealing, working with several different guys and crews at the same time. One guy he stole with we called Mousey. When Mousey got arrested and locked up, Tony said he felt bad and wanted to help Mousey's wife out while he was in jail. I took Tony over to Mousey's place and introduced him to her. He started stopping in with groceries for her and gave her some cash on occasion.

One day Tony told me, "Frankie, I fucked up again, as usual."

"What are you talking about?"

"Mousey's wife. I've been banging her."

"Tony, that's wrong. He's your fuckin' partner."

"I know. I said, 'I fucked up.' She was lonely so I tried to comfort her, and it just happened. When it comes to women, I just can't control myself."

That was Tony.

* * *

When I was around twenty or twenty-one, there was a guy in Chicago I used to steal with named Phil Manzella. Phil was married and was very jealous.

Tony and I were in a tavern in Elmwood Park one afternoon when Phil and his wife came in and sat across the bar from us. I thought she looked scared. We waved, and Phil came over to talk.

He said, "I'm having a lot of problems with my old lady. She wants to leave me, and I won't let her go. This is the first time I've had her out of the house in months."

I said, "What do you mean she hasn't been out of the house in months?"

"That's right. I keep her tied up. I let her out today because she promised she'd be good."

"You're crazy," I said. "That's kidnapping."

He shrugged. "She's my wife, and I can do what I want to do."

Phil returned to his seat, and a few minutes later he and his wife started arguing. It got pretty loud. He tried to pull her off the stool to leave, but she wouldn't go.

She screamed at him, "I'm not leaving. You've had me tied to the bed posts for weeks. I'm loose now, and I'm not going back!"

Tony said to me, "What do you think we should do?"

"I don't think we should get involved. Phil's nuts. He might have a gun and shoot us both if we go over there."

Phil went to the pay phone and called his mother. She lived a few blocks away and came right over. She tried to pull her daughter-in-law off the stool, with no luck.

The bartender went over and told Phil and his mother to leave. When they refused he said he was going to call the cops. At that point they left, but Phil said he'd be waiting outside. Tony and I went out to talk with him.

Tony said, "Phil, you've gotta get out of here before the cops come, or you and your mother might both get locked up. Frankie and I will talk to your wife and bring her home to you."

When we went inside Phil's wife told us her side of the story.

She said, "He ties my ankles and wrists to the bed posts and rapes me constantly. He's dangerous, and I'm scared. I won't go back to that house. Will you help me?"

We agreed to put her up at a motel. We got her a room, gave her a few bucks, and left.

A few blocks from the motel, Tony said, "Frankie, turn around and take me back to the motel."

"What for?"

"She's scared and shouldn't be left alone. Take me back, and I'll spend some time with her."

I knew what that meant, but I took him back to the motel

anyway.

Tony called me the next afternoon and asked me to pick him up. When he got in the car I asked him what was going on.

He said, "Her parents live out of state. She called them, and they're coming to get her. I paid the room for a week and gave her some money. She's all set until they get here."

"Did you bang her?"

He laughed. "Of course. I gave her $500, though. That's more than a good hooker costs."

Phil put the word out that he thought Tony and I had screwed his wife and he wasn't happy about it, but he didn't take any action.

Then in 1967, Phil murdered two of his former in-laws. He went on the lam and left word behind that he was gonna kill me and Tony now that he had nothing to lose. We kept our eyes open, but he never showed up.

The law caught up with him in Texas, dressed as a woman. They brought him back to Illinois, convicted him of the murders, and gave him a life sentence. He died in prison.

* * *

Tony couldn't help being a womanizer, and being married to Nancy didn't slow him down. In fact, when I joined him in Las Vegas in 1979, he not only had his wife but two steady girlfriends, besides. (I'll call them Mary and Sally.) And he was always looking for more. I don't think it's a stretch to say that Tony wanted to have sex with about any decent-looking woman he laid eyes on.

To make my point, when I arrived in Vegas I had a good-looking girl with me who planned to make money hooking. Tony saw her and took an interest.

He said, "I'd sure like to get some of that."

I joked, "Not with her. You'd spoil her if you ever put that thing you got into her."

He didn't ask about her again.

* * *

Nancy Spilotro knew what Tony did for a living, but she also viewed him as a husband and father. In a 2004 interview with my co-author Denny Griffin, she said:

"Tony was a regular guy. He liked home cooking, and we seldom ate out. Tony always fixed Vincent breakfast (usually pancakes). We seldom went to the Strip unless there was a special show we wanted to see or if we had out-of-town company. We visited Disneyland from time-to-time, where Tony's favorite ride was It's A Small World. *The Sound of Music*, with Julie Andrews, was his favorite movie."

Nancy was a petite woman. She was also very jealous of Tony, and although she was small, she was a spitfire. She knew in her heart he was cheating on her, but she could never catch him at it.

Mary and Sally were both very attractive and had legitimate jobs. The funny thing was they didn't know about each other. Tony took care of them physically and financially, too, when they needed help.

When Mary—a single mother—got into a scrape with the IRS and owed them several thousand dollars, Tony gave her the money she needed to settle the debt with no questions asked. He told me he thought the IRS was pressuring her to get to him, and he felt a little guilty. Paying off the bill made him feel better, plus it got her out from under the G-men.

Tony told me a story about the day he was having sex with Mary at his Gold Rush jewelry store when Nancy showed up. He rushed Mary up to a small room in the attic and then buzzed Nancy inside.

"What are you doing here?" he asked.

"I know you've got a woman here with you."

"Come on, honey. You can see there's nobody here but you and me."

He calmed her down, and she left.

I told him he'd get caught someday. It was just a matter of time.

* * *

I hadn't been in Vegas very long when another guy, named Leo Guardino, and I partnered up to open an Italian restaurant. We found a location at 4110 South Maryland Parkway that could be remodeled. We had to come up with $65,000 and had the money together after only three residential burglaries. The name we picked for the place was Upper Crust. An adjoining business was a bar called My Place Lounge. Both places became hangouts for Tony Spilotro and other Vegas wiseguys.

One day Tony came into the restaurant and said he'd just had a big fight with Nancy. I asked him what it was about.

He said, "I was in bed sleeping. When I woke up she was standing next to the bed with a .38 snub-nose pointing at me. [It was very similar to the scene between Henry Hill and his wife in the movie *Goodfellas.*] I asked her what the hell was going on. She said she knew I had a girlfriend and was going to blow my brains out.

"I got out of bed real slow and talked to her calmly as I walked toward her. When I got close enough, I grabbed the gun and took it away from her. I told her if she ever did that again, I'd kill her."

A half-hour or so later, Nancy burst in the door. She started yelling at Tony. He went outside and stood by her car. She followed him.

"You motherfucker!" she screamed. "I know you've got a girlfriend. I'm going to kill you, you bastard!"

What happened next was hilarious. Nancy went to hit Tony, and he ran. He didn't run away, though—he ran around the car and she chased him. Here was the great Tony Spilotro—considered at the time to be the most dangerous man in Las Vegas—being chased around a car by a four-foot-ten-inch, hundred-pound lady.

It was even funnier because poor Nancy thought he only had one girlfriend—little did she know.

* * *

Of all Tony's affairs, the one that caused him the most trouble was the one with Lefty Rosenthal's wife, Geri. The Outfit frowned on members or associates getting involved with the wives of other mobsters. It was even more serious in Lefty's case, because he was a valuable asset to them.

I found out about their relationship when Geri stopped at the Upper Crust looking for Tony. She seemed upset and said, "Where's Tony? I've got to talk to him right away."

Tony was next door at the My Place, so I told her a semi-lie. "He's not here right now. I can try to find him for you if you want."

"Please. It's very important."

I went next door and told Tony, "Geri Rosenthal's in the restaurant looking for you."

"What the fuck does she want?"

"I don't know. She only said it's real important that she talk with you."

Tony went to get Geri and brought her back to the lounge. Half an hour later she left.

Afterward, he came into the Upper Crust, shaking his head.

He said to me, "Boy, have I fucked up this time, Frankie. I've been banging that broad, and I shouldn't have. You know how it is. She and Lefty were having problems. She came to me for help—even asked me to kill him. I've got no respect for that Jew, but I told her there was no way I could kill him. She cried a little, and I tried to comfort her. The next thing I knew we were in bed.

"Now she told me that her and Lefty were arguing and

she admitted to him that I'm fucking her. If this ever gets back to Chicago I'll have nothing but headaches."

I said, "The Outfit's got millions of dollars invested in these casinos. They aren't going to be very happy if they think you've done anything to screw it up. We might end up with a war on our hands, and we could lose."

The next trip I made to Chicago to deliver the Outfit's tribute money, Joe Ferriola, one of the bosses, wanted to talk to me.

He said, "Frankie, you've gotta level with me. Is the Little Guy fucking the Jew's wife?"

"No way." I lied. "I know Tony and Lefty aren't getting along, but as far as I know Tony's not banging Lefty's old lady."

"I believe you. You know we've got a lot of money riding out there, and we can't have things get fucked up just because some guy gets a hard-on. If that happens, a lot of people will be mad, including me."

Nothing happened right away, but I think it came back to bite Tony later. When the Outfit whacked him in 1986, Ferriola was the acting boss and approved the hit. I have a feeling he knew the truth, and that was one of the things on his mind when he gave the okay.

7

RONNIE DEANGELO

Ronnie DeAngelo was a valuable asset to the Outfit. He was a genius with his hands and could make almost anything criminals needed to do scores, hits, and monitor the police. He worked for Felix "Milwaukee Phil" Alderisio among others and helped Tony and me out a lot. He also did a special personal job for Tony that I'll tell you about shortly.

I first met Ronnie when I was trying to figure a way to keep track of what the cops were up to while my crew and I were doing burglaries. I wanted something portable we could take into the building with us. That way if we heard the cops were coming we could contact our getaway driver by walkie-talkie and he'd pick us up. This was before police scanners existed and even before the cops had portable radios. I talked with Tony about it, and he said, "There's only one guy I know who might be able to fix you up with something like that." He introduced me to Ronnie.

I explained to Ronnie what I wanted and why. I said, "It has to be small, portable, and easy to conceal."

"How small?" he asked.

"I want the radio to be able to fit inside a camera case."

We looked through several radio books, and Ronnie thought about it for a while, then his face broke into a smile. "I can do it. All I'll have to do is build circuit boards."

In those days the radios required crystals with the correct frequency. I had Ronnie build the radios to hold three crystals, so we could listen in to the dispatch frequencies of three different police agencies by just switching channels. The radios were powered by four standard batteries. Thanks to Ronnie, my crew could have a guy outside in the car listening to police calls while the rest of the guys were inside the building doing the score. I was really impressed with him, and that was just the beginning.

Ronnie also modified our cars by adding hidden compartments where we could stash stolen goods (such as jewelry), cash and weapons. If you needed a silencer for your gun, he'd make one for you. And if you needed a bomb to blow something or somebody up, you went to Ronnie.

In addition to being very intelligent, Ronnie was also a good-looking guy.

* * *

Now I'll tell you about the personal thing Ronnie did for Tony. I don't remember the exact year, but it had to be in 1964 or '65. I was parked in front of a restaurant in Chicago talking with a girl named Sandy Porter. She was a close friend of my ex-wife, very attractive and kind of wild. In fact, later on I ended up doing time for a robbery her boyfriend did that got hung on me.

Anyway, Tony pulled up and came over to my car. I introduced him to Sandy, and the three of us talked for several minutes. Finally, Tony said, "I'd like to talk with Sandy alone, do you mind?"

I figured he was going to make a move on her. I wanted to give him a heads up that she wasn't married and had a kid about a year old, but there was no way I could do it in front of her.

I said, "No, I don't mind. Go ahead."

Sandy and Tony went to his car and talked for quite a while. He walked her back to my car, and as she got in he said, "I've gotta get going. She'll tell you what this is about."

After Tony left, Sandy said, "We had a nice talk, and he offered me a job."

"You don't have to tell me, it's none of my business."

"That's okay; I want to tell you. Tony said he'll pay me $10,000 to have sex with some guy named Ronnie DeAngelo and have a baby. Tony and his wife will adopt the kid right away, and it doesn't matter if it's a boy or girl."

I knew Tony and Nancy wanted a child but couldn't have one—as I recall it was Tony who was sterile. When I suggested they adopt one he said that with his background none of the adoption agencies would approve him. It looked like he'd decided to take control of things, have surrogate parents, and adopt the baby privately.

"Are you going to do it?"

"I probably will. I told him to call me in a couple of days, and I'd give him my answer."

"I think it would be a good thing. I know for sure Tony and Nancy would be great parents."

Sandy and Ronnie got together shortly afterward, and I believe Vincent was born about a year later—I'm pretty sure it was in 1966. As promised, Tony adopted the baby right away. I never asked Ronnie about the financial arrangements, but I assume he was paid ten grand, too. Everybody was happy, and Tony adored the kid.

When I talked with Sandy later she said she was glad she did it, although after having Vincent it was a little tough to give him up. Knowing he was going to a good home made it easier, though. I continued to see Sandy around once in a while, but that was the last time she mentioned Vincent until I moved to Vegas.

I was still getting settled into my apartment when Sandy called. She said, "Frankie, I don't know how to reach Tony directly. Can you deliver a message for me?"

"Sure. What do you want me to tell him?"

"Let him know that I'd like to move to Vegas if I can get a good job there. I know Tony has a lot of pull and can probably line something up for me. When you talk to him, remind him that he owes me."

"Are you sure you want me to tell him that?"

"Yeah, just like I said."

I saw Tony a couple days later and delivered Sandy's message. When I said she wanted to make sure I told him he owed her, it didn't go over very well.

Tony's expression was very serious. "Tell that motherfucker if she ever tries to blackmail me again she won't have to worry about employment."

I called Sandy and just told her it wouldn't be a very good idea for her to come to Vegas. She must have read between the lines because I never saw or heard from her again.

Ronnie did come to Vegas to visit, and Tony brought him to my Upper Crust restaurant to see me. When I saw him I was surprised and said, "What the hell are you doing here?"

He smiled. "I came to see the kid."

I never talked to Ronnie about being Vincent's father, but it was obvious to me he was aware that I knew.

I don't know if Sandy is still alive. Ronnie ended up committing suicide when he found out he had terminal cancer. I'm pretty sure Nancy knew all the details of the adoption, but I don't know whether Tony ever told Vincent who his biological parents were.

8

A FUTURE BOSS

Events took place that would impact Tony Spilotro's life even before he was born and while he was a young boy. In this chapter I'm going to tell you about them and how they affected Tony's rise through the Outfit ranks, leading to him eventually becoming the boss of Las Vegas, Southern California, and Arizona. I'll begin with some well-documented history and will include my personal knowledge and opinions where appropriate.

Most organized crime enthusiasts are well aware of Bugsy Siegel's role in the development of Las Vegas. Bugsy was a New York guy and an associate of Lucky Luciano and Meyer Lansky.

A lesser known name that is also connected to the early days of Mob influence in Vegas is Marshall Caifano. He was from Chicago and had worked for Al Capone and Frank Nitti. The five-foot, five-inch Caifano was suspected of numerous murders and known as a "do whatever it takes" kind of guy. Sound familiar?

Following Bugsy's murder in 1947, Johnny Roselli became Chicago's representative in Los Angeles, Hollywood, and Las Vegas. During that same time period Caifano took care of many of Chicago's West Coast enforcement matters. However, by the late 1950s the Outfit—then under the leadership of Sam Giancana—decided its growing Las Vegas casino interests required the on-site presence of a highly skilled enforcer, and in 1958 Giancana assigned Marshall Caifano to be the Outfit's "outside man" in Sin City. His job was to assist the Outfit's "inside men" (those managing the casinos they controlled) in preventing pilferage of the money that was being skimmed from the casinos and deter interlopers from other crime families from muscling in. Accomplishing those tasks could require anything from intimidation and verbal threats to physical beatings and murder.

Caifano wasn't awarded the plum job just because of his talents, though. Giancana had another motive for selecting him: the boss was having an affair with Caifano's wife. Sending her husband to Nevada while she remained in Chicago would make things much easier for the lovers.

When an FBI agent confronted Caifano with the affair in an attempt to flip him, the killer didn't fly into a rage and threaten to kill Giancana, which would have been justified under Mob protocol. Instead, his response was a laugh and a big smile. Apparently he felt that allowing his wife to sleep with Giancana was a career enhancer.

I knew Caifano from my neighborhood, and Tony knew him through the Outfit. Tony described him as "a man's man." Coming from Tony, that was high praise.

After I rolled and became a government witness in 1982 the feds told me they visited Caifano, who was then in prison. He said to the agents, "I suppose you're here because Cullotta rolled?"

"Yeah, we know you two were associated and thought maybe you'd like to help us out, too."

The agent told me, "He just smiled and said, 'Tell Frankie I said good luck.'"

* * *

Another major player of the day was Paul Ricca. He was born in Italy in 1897 and at the age of seventeen committed his first Mafia hit, for which he served two years in prison. After his release, Ricca murdered a witness who had testified against him and then fled to the United States, arriving on August 10, 1920, and eventually settled in Chicago. Ricca later hooked up with what was known as the 42 Gang, a group of young thieves and street toughs from the neighborhood known as "the Patch." The gang served as kind of a farm team for Al Capone's operation, which would become known as the Outfit. With the exception of Tony Accardo, almost everybody who was anybody in the Outfit in those days was a 42 member.

When Capone went to prison for tax evasion in 1931, Ricca, Frank Nitti, and future boss Tony Accardo formed a ruling panel to run the organization. They utilized their fellow Capone associate Murray "The Camel" Humphreys, a top labor and political racketeer, to corrupt politicians and gain influence with labor unions.

They quickly infiltrated the International Alliance of Theatrical Stage Employees and Motion Picture Operators union in Hollywood. Using their control of the union they conspired to extort a million dollars from four Hollywood movie studios. When the scheme was discovered, Ricca and seven others were charged and convicted. Ricca was sentenced to ten years in prison and was released in August 1947.

From there, Ricca along with Accardo went on to become two of the most powerful men in Chicago organized crime. Although Accardo received most of the recognition as being the boss, Ricca was his equal in power and authority.

After Giancana got into legal trouble in 1966, Joe Aiuppa became the boss of record, but I heard stories that Ricca and Accardo were actually running things. One day I asked Tony who the real head of the Outfit was. He said, "Ricca is the guy, Accardo advises him, and Aiuppa is the figurehead."

* * *

Prior to making his bones with the Outfit, Tony's first major position was as an enforcer and collector for the sadistic Outfit-connected bookie and loan shark Sam "Mad Sam" DeStefano, a top Mob earner. Although Sam made a lot of money for the Outfit, he was known to be a loose cannon. Because of that, Paul Ricca wanted someone who could be trusted to go to work for Sam, keep an eye on him, and hopefully keep him from getting too far out of line. Tony Spilotro got the job.

I'm going to tell you the following story to give you an idea of what kind of guy Sam was.

One day Tony stopped at my house and said, "Take a ride with me."

"What's up?"

"Sam's having trouble with a lawyer he uses sometimes named McDonald. He wants me to scoop McDonald up and bring him to his house so he can teach him a lesson. The guy's afraid of Sam, so we've got to bullshit him and say it's no big deal and that Sam just wants to talk with him."

We found McDonald in a restaurant on Roosevelt Road that a lot of lawyers hung out at. Tony gave him the line that there was nothing wrong, and McDonald went with us. It was all laughing and joking on the way to Sam's house on Harlem Avenue. We took McDonald down to the basement, and he still didn't have a clue as to what was going on.

When Sam came down the stairs Tony and I grabbed McDonald and tied him to a chair. Then Sam started to work on him, beating him and urinating on him. I knew Sam's nickname was "Mad Sam," and his performance that day convinced me he was a lunatic.

When Sam was satisfied he said to McDonald, "I'm not going to kill you today, but if you ever fuck me up again you're a dead man. Now, thank me for not killing you."

McDonald said in a shaky voice, "Thank you, Sam, for not killing me."

I couldn't help but think of that Robin Dragon kid thanking Tony for not killing him.

We untied McDonald and drove him to his car in the parking lot of the restaurant. He did get whacked later on, but I don't know for sure who did it. I figure it was probably Sam himself or someone acting on his orders.

This is just one example of Sam's depravity, and you'll

hear more about him in the pages ahead.

It was while Tony was working for Sam that an opportunity arose that I believe resulted in his becoming a "made member" of the Outfit and eventually to him being assigned their man in Vegas. The incident became known as the M&M Murders.

9

THE M&M MURDERS

In 1962, I was stealing with a couple of guys named Billy McCarthy and Jimmy Miraglia. They were good thieves, and we were making some big scores. We operated independent of Tony and the Outfit.

One night, I think it was in May, Billy was out drinking by himself and went into a saloon in Rosemont called the Black Door. The joint was owned by Frank Pondeleo, an associate of Outfit boss Paul "the Waiter" Ricca. Two brothers, Ronnie and Phil Scalvo, managed it for Pondeleo. Their father was closely tied to the big boss, Tony Accardo.

Billy got into an argument with Ronnie that turned into a fistfight. Ronnie and Phil beat up Billy and threw him out. Billy was pissed off, and a few nights later he and Jimmy went to the bar to teach the Scalvo brothers a lesson. Instead of getting even, they both got roughed up and tossed out. They came to me afterward looking for help in getting revenge.

"Those fuckin' Scalvos went too far this time," Billy said. "A beatin' is too good for 'em now; they gotta be killed. Are you with us, Frankie?"

"I know how you feel, Billy, but you've gotta forget about it. That place is connected, and you can't fuck around with those guys. If we do anything to the Scalvos we'll all end up gettin' whacked."

"Come on, Frankie, I know you. If you were in our shoes, those bastards would be dead already. How about it?"

I wasn't real excited about it, but Billy and Jimmy were my guys so I said I'd help them with the killings. But it was understood we wouldn't hit the Scalvos at the bar or in a Mob-controlled neighborhood.

We started watching the Black Door around closing time, figuring when the brothers left we could follow them to neutral turf and do the job. But every time they came out they had the cocktail waitress with them. I said I didn't want any part of killing an innocent bystander. We agreed we'd watch the place every so often until the right opportunity came along.

One night when I was at the bowling alley on a date, Billy came in and asked, "Are you ready to take care of that business tonight?"

I knew he was talking about the Scalvos. I said, "I've been trying to get into this broad's pants for months, can we go another time?"

"That's okay," Billy said. "Stay here and Jimmy and I will go. Are the guns in your garage?"

"Yeah, the side door is open."

Jimmy and Billy went to the Black Door without me. They ended up following the Scalvos and the waitress when they left the bar. They tailed them for about seven miles to Elmwood Park (a heavily Mob-connected area), and when the Scalvos parked on a side street, Billy and Jimmy killed all three of them—the brothers and the waitress.

The bosses went nuts and put the word out that justice was going to be done. The murderers were under a death sentence. Whoever identified and dealt with the killers would make his bones with the Outfit.

Tony, still working for Mad Sam, rightly figured if he could resolve the Scalvo murders, he'd be rewarded by becoming a made member of the Outfit. A couple of days later he paid me a visit.

"I know you hang out with Billy and Jimmy," Tony said. "They had a problem with the Scalvo brothers, and now the Scalvos are dead, along with a waitress. They [the Outfit] think you, Billy, and Jimmy were the hit men."

"I had nothing to do with that, Tony, absolutely nothing."

"Look, Frankie, I've been stickin' up for you with these people. I personally guaranteed them you weren't there, that if you knew anything you'd tell me, huh? But here's the way it is. You've got to give up Billy and Jimmy. If you don't, I can't save you."

That was that. If I tried to cover for Billy and Jimmy, I'd be dead, too. What choice did I have? I told Tony the whole story.

"You done the right thing, Frankie. Those guys fucked up bad, and now they have to pay. But you've got no problem; you're going to be okay."

Two days later, Tony asked me to meet him at a bowling alley I hung out at. I figured he'd want me to set up Billy and Jimmy. I was right.

"They [the bosses] want to talk with Billy McCarthy, and they need your help in making the arrangements," Tony said.

"What do you want me to do?"

"Call Billy and ask him to meet you at the North Avenue Chicken House at eight o'clock tonight."

I got on the payphone and called Billy's house. His wife, Betty, answered and put him on the line. I scheduled the meet while Tony stood next to me and listened.

"Good job, Frankie. Meet me at the Howard Johnson's on North Avenue at 7:45. Make sure you drive your own car."

That night I met Tony and Outfit guy Vincent "Saint" Inserro at the Howard Johnson's. Tony took my car and left me with Saint in their car. Saint popped his front radio speaker and pulled out a .38. I turned toward him, and my right hand went behind my back where I had a gun in my waistband. He saw my move and lowered his own gun to a less threatening position between his legs.

About forty minutes later, Tony returned. He said, "Here's your car, Frankie. See you later." I heard him tell Saint there hadn't been any problems.

The following morning Billy's wife called me. "Where's Billy?"

"I don't know. He never showed up last night."

"Something's wrong, I know it. He drove my father's car, and he'd never be gone all night unless something happened."

"I'll check around and keep my ears open. I'll call you if I hear anything."

That was the last time I talked with her.

I thought Billy was probably dead, and Tony confirmed that when we talked about ten days later.

"Billy's wife called me a few days ago lookin' for him," I said.

"Frankie, Billy's gone. It's all over. Forget about it; it's done. I don't want you to say anything to Jimmy about it, though."

"Can you tell me what happened that night at the Chicken House?"

"I guess so. Billy was in the restaurant looking for you. I told him you were outside waiting for him. I said, 'Let's go see him.' When we got outside, Billy saw the Outfit guys and went for his gun. I grabbed him around the neck and shoved him in the Outfit car. He went rather easily, Frankie."

I saw Jimmy in a restaurant a few nights later. "Have you seen Billy around?" I asked.

"No, no I haven't. Why?"

"Don't you think that's kind of strange? Maybe you ought to make yourself scarce."

"I'm not worried. I haven't done anything wrong."

I learned that the very next night Jimmy went to a lounge in Chicago. Felix "Milwaukee Phil" Alderisio, Chuckie Nicoletti, and some other Outfit guys were outside in their work car, laying for him. Jimmy got lucky when the police spotted the car and searched it. They found a stash of guns and arrested everybody. That should have been another message for Jimmy, and he should have run like hell right then, but he didn't. They got him the next day.

Tony told me all about it shortly afterward.

"Phil [Alderisio], Turk [Torello], Saint, and me found

Jimmy in a lounge in Niles [a Chicago suburb]. We took him in the liquor storage room and beat him, but we didn't kill him. We left him locked in the room, and while we were gone, Jimmy got into the booze. He was drunk when we came back for him and was makin' a lot of noise, so we beat him again to shut him up. One of the punches caught him in the throat and must have got his voice box, because after that he could barely talk.

"We took him out and put him in the trunk of his car to take him to join Billy. Saint and I were in the follow car. While we were drivin' Jimmy apparently pulled out the wires for the brake lights. When we saw the brake lights in his car go out we called Phil and Turk on the walkie-talkie and told them to pull over so we could find out what the problem was. As soon as we opened the trunk Jimmy jumped out and made a run for it. We caught him, knocked him out, and put him back in the trunk.

"When we got to Billy's car Jimmy was awake. He knew he was going to be killed and asked to be strangled so his wife could collect some insurance money. We strangled him right there while he was still in the trunk and dumped his body in with Billy's. Then we drove the car to another neighborhood and ditched it. A couple of days later somebody noticed the stench and called the cops."

Tony was in a talkative mood that day and told me the rest of the story about the night Billy McCarthy was killed. After they grabbed him at the Chicken House they took him to the basement of a house in Cicero.

"He was one tough fuckin' Irishman. We beat that motherfucker with everything, but he wouldn't tell us who did the Scalvos with him. We finally got so pissed off we put his head in a vise and turned it. The kid's eyeball popped right out of his fuckin' head. Billy begged me to kill him. He gave up Jimmy's name just before he died."

The killings of Billy and Jimmy became known as the M&M Murders. There was even a scene in the 1995 movie

Casino based on Billy's death in which actor Joe Pesci's character placed a man's head in a vise and squeezed until an eyeball popped out.

Tony was right. Billy was a tough fucking Irishman.

10

REWARDED

The M&M killings endeared Tony to Paul Ricca, and with Ricca's support, Tony's rise to a top spot was assured. And Ricca wasn't Tony's only ally. His associations with the likes of Felix "Milwaukee Phil" Alderisio, hit man Frankie "The German" Schweihs, James "Turk" Torello, and Joey Lombardo put him in good stead throughout most of his criminal career, before Lombardo turned on him at the end.

* * *

While Tony was on the rise in Chicago, Marshall Caifano—who was similar to Tony in physical stature and temperament—was on the downslide in Las Vegas.

In an effort to crack down on organized crime's influence in the casino business, Nevada had taken steps to ban undesirables from being anywhere on casino property, including restaurants, bars, and showrooms. Their names were placed in what was commonly known as the "Black Book." People whose names made it into the Book could be arrested if found in violation of the ban, and the owners of the properties on which they were found could be fined and eventually lose their license to operate. Marshall Caifano was "Booked" in 1960, and he didn't like it. He continued to prowl the Strip and was arrested after entering the Stardust three times in one night.

Following that, Caifano sued Nevada, challenging their right to name him an excluded person. He lost the case and his name stayed in the Book, but the entire episode got the attention of Ricca and Accardo in a very negative way. They wanted their operatives to fly under the radar and knew that flaunting the law and filing lawsuits was not the way to do it.

Ricca instructed Giancana to replace Caifano with

Roselli until a permanent replacement could be found. As ordered, Giancana recalled Caifano from Vegas, and Roselli was again the Outfit's man there. That arrangement lasted until 1967, when Roselli was indicted for his role in a card-cheating scam at the Friars Club in Los Angeles. He was convicted at trial and sentenced to five years in prison.

The Las Vegas position was open yet again, and Paul Ricca had to decide who was going to fill it. He chose a man with many of the same qualities as Marshall Caifano. A man who had proved his loyalty to the Outfit over many years and who in 1962 had avenged an atrocity that took place against a Ricca-owned business. He selected Tony Spilotro.

So in 1971, Tony, Nancy, and Vincent moved to Las Vegas. Tony's boss back in Chicago was his long-time friend Turk Torello, and when Torello died in 1979, Joey Lombardo became Tony's immediate supervisor.

In October 1972, just a few months after Tony assumed his new role in Las Vegas, Paul Ricca died of a heart attack.

Back in Chicago, Marshall Caifano was credited with luring rogue Chicago detective Richard Cain to Rosie's Sandwich Shop on December 20, 1973, where Cain was gunned down by masked assassins. In 1980, Caifano was convicted on federal charges of transporting stolen securities and served ten years in prison. He died in 2003 of natural causes.

* * *

Tony Spilotro had realized his dream of becoming a powerful Outfit leader and was in charge of the Outfit's operations in Las Vegas, Arizona, and California. Some people would have been satisfied with such a coveted position, but not Tony. He was determined to expand on his authority and build his own empire.

11

BODY COUNT

So far I've told you Tony roughed up some people and killed a couple. Some of you might be inclined to think Tony was a tough guy and a crook but wasn't really the cold-blooded killer portrayed by actor Joe Pesci in *Casino*. I can't let you leave Chicago with those thoughts in your mind. So I'm going to close this section by telling you about the other murders Tony was involved in or suspected of while still in the Windy City in the 1960s and before I joined him in Vegas in 1979. Some of them are clean kills, but I think others were more brutal than they needed to be—such as Action Jackson. And there are probably more killings I don't know about.

Anyway, here they are, year-by-year with the details as I know them. You will note that most of the killings were never solved.

William 'Action' Jackson

In the early 1960s Tony Spilotro was an up-and-coming mobster and was making quite a name for himself providing muscle for a connected Chicago loan shark "Mad Sam" DeStefano. Sam was widely known as a sadistic bastard that liked to torture people he thought had crossed him, and even murdered his own brother on the Outfit's orders.

One of Sam's collectors was a guy named William "Action" Jackson. He was a very big man, going 300 pounds or more and had once worked as a bouncer at a local lounge. Sam thought Jackson was stealing from him, which was a very bad thing. Besides that, Jackson had been indicted on a federal hijacking charge and was rumored to be trying to make a deal with the feds. Not surprisingly, his body was found stuffed in the trunk of his car on August 11, 1961.

The reports were that Jackson had been brutally tortured before he died. To me, that confirmed the word on the street that Sam was behind the murder. And knowing that Tony was part of Sam's muscle, I figured he probably had a hand in it, too.

A few weeks after Jackson's body was found, I was talking with Tony and mentioned the murder.

"Yeah, he was doing some loan sharking for Sam, and he was playin' with the money. Maybe he was thinking about working with the G [FBI], too. You fuck around like that you get in trouble. And with a guy like Sam there are no second chances. He wanted him dead, and that was that."

"He was a big fuckin' guy, Tony. Sam could never take him down alone."

Tony laughed. "He had plenty of help. Me, Chuckie [Grimaldi], Saint [Inserro], and Dicky [Gorman] scooped him up off the street. We held guns on him but bullshitted him into thinking we just wanted to take him somewhere to talk about the money he was short and then everything would be okay.

"We took him to this meat plant owned by friends of Sam's. When we got him there we tied him up, and then Sam came in. I think right then he knew he was a dead man."

"But according to the papers he was beaten, burned, and stabbed. Why not just kill him?"

"That's not the way Sam does things, Frankie. He figures killing guys that way sends a message and makes people fear him. Plus, he enjoys it. And I gotta tell you I never seen anything like it before.

"We hung him on a meat hook like they put dead cows on. Sam used a blowtorch on him, a cattle prod, ice picked him in the balls, and shot him in the kneecap. The fuckin' guy finally had a heart attack and died. And that really pissed Sam off because he wasn't finished with him yet."

Action Jackson was the first murder I ever knew for sure Tony was involved with. I was a little disappointed that he went in for the torture stuff, though. I always believed that if you had to whack somebody, just do it and get it over with.

But Tony was determined to go places in the Outfit and was willing to do whatever it took to get there, even if it meant being part of that kind of thing.

So Mad Sam found a diamond in the rough when Tony went to work for him. He taught his protégé how to make money and that you had to be totally ruthless to get power and hold on to it. They were lessons Tony learned well and would eventually come back on Sam, himself.

* * *

Marilyn Monroe

Not long after my book *CULLOTTA* was published in 2007, my writer, Denny Griffin, called me. He said a guy from Louisiana, who claimed to be working on an organized crime documentary, had contacted him wanting to set up an interview with me. When Denny pinned him down for specifics, the guy said he had information that Tony Spilotro and I murdered Marilyn Monroe and he'd like to talk with me about it. I wasn't interested and told Denny to tell him thanks but no thanks.

That was the first time I heard my name tossed around as Monroe's killer. But it wasn't the only time Tony was mentioned. I know I had nothing to do with her death, and I don't believe Tony did either. Before I tell you why, I want to make sure you understand that, officially, Monroe's death was determined to be a suicide or possibly an accident, resulting from a self-administered drug overdose. There was no murder. You can believe that if you want. I don't.

Why do I think the official record is wrong? Let's look at some facts.

To begin with, think about who Monroe was involved with: John and Bobby Kennedy and Sam Giancana, for starters. John was president of the United States, and his brother Bobby was his attorney general. Sam Giancana was boss of the Chicago Outfit. Some very powerful people.

Also, it's well known that Giancana was instrumental in getting John elected by having the Chicago Mob get out the vote for him. Kennedy carried Chicago and won Illinois, putting him in the White House. Another fact that's pretty much undisputed is that Monroe was sleeping with John and Bobby, both of whom were married Catholics, and Giancana made the introductions.

You have to remember we're talking about the early 1960s, when attitudes about adultery were a lot different than they are today—especially among Catholics. Back then, a sex scandal involving the Kennedys had the potential to do a lot of damage and maybe even destroy John's presidency.

So in 1962 Marilyn Monroe is sleeping with and hanging out with people that have tremendous power and, because of that, a lot to lose. In addition to the affairs, she's seen and overheard a lot of things that could be embarrassing or worse. She has to be kept on the reservation.

But Monroe is frustrated that her relationships with the Kennedys aren't going anywhere and, on top of that, she's using drugs. She starts making threats about going to the press and blowing the whistle. And if she does, it could bring down the Kennedys and who knows how many others.

For Monroe to commit suicide or die by accident at that time would have been convenient. But with all that was at stake, her fate couldn't be left to chance. I believe when she threatened to go public she signed her own death warrant.

Under the circumstances, when she was found dead in her home that August, most of the guys I knew weren't surprised. And none of us thought it was an accident.

Since then, there have been all kinds of theories floated about who ordered Monroe's murder. Was it John or Bobby? Maybe it was Giancana. Remember, she knew enough about the relationship between John and him to open a big can of worms for him and the Outfit. All the players had reasons to want to see Monroe's mouth closed for good, or so it seemed.

I don't believe the Outfit had a role in Monroe's death,

though. The only reason I don't believe they were involved is because JFK had reneged on the promises Joe Kennedy made to Giancana when he asked for help in getting his son elected. Instead of being friendly to the Mob, he made Bobby the top cop and told him to lock us all up. So contrary to the speculation that Giancana ordered Monroe killed to protect the Kennedys, the Outfit was in no mood to do the Kennedy boys any favors.

Under the circumstances, I don't see any way Giancana would have stuck his neck out to help them and face all the heat knocking off a celebrity like Monroe would bring. And think about this. If Monroe talked and the Kennedy regime came crashing down, John and Bobby would be out of power and the heat would be off. So, in a way, the Outfit would be better off if she stayed alive.

Even though I didn't think it was an Outfit job, I did ask Tony about it. He dismissed it with a laugh, saying, "I'll tell ya, Frankie, if fuckin' Donald Duck got whacked today they'd blame the Outfit or me for it."

If the Mob didn't kill Monroe, who did? Here's what I think happened.

The Kennedy family had the money and connections to do whatever they wanted. John and Bobby were probably the start of a political dynasty, and neither Marilyn Monroe nor anybody else was going to stand in the way. When it became clear that she was out of control and ready to go public, John and Bobby—and maybe their father—agreed she had to go and made the arrangements to make it happen. Whoever did the job was smart and took advantage of Monroe's drug habit to make her death appear to be a suicide or accident. It worked.

I'm sorry if I disappointed those of you who thought Monroe was a Mob hit. In my opinion she was murdered, but not by the Outfit.

* * *

Leo Foreman

A murder Dicky Gorman confirmed to me—one for which Tony got indicted—was that of Leo Foreman, another of Mad Sam DeStefano's collectors. Dicky wasn't in on the killing, but Tony told him about.

Foreman held a legit job as a real estate agent and worked for Sam on the side. Similar to Action Jackson, Foreman was a big guy—six feet, two inches tall and 270 pounds. According to reports, he got on Sam's bad side initially because of a traffic ticket Sam received. Instead of simply paying the fine, Sam decided to fight the ticket and went to trial where he knew Foreman was a friend of the judge.

Sam acted as his own attorney, and his misconduct in the courtroom resulted in the supposedly friendly judge holding him in contempt and imposing a fine of several hundred dollars. Even though he was found innocent of the traffic charge, Sam was embarrassed over the contempt finding and went into a rage because Foreman hadn't done more to put the judge firmly in his corner. Foreman was on thin ice with Sam and needed to be extra careful not to further antagonize him. But he wasn't.

Not long after the court thing, Sam discovered Foreman was shorting him on his collections. When he went to Foreman's real estate office and confronted him, Foreman admitted that his math might have been a little bit off, but it was no big deal. That attitude sent Sam into a screaming frenzy, causing Foreman to pull a gun and order him out.

After the argument with Sam, Foreman must have figured he'd made a bad mistake because he kept clear of Sam for weeks. But Sam had a plan to get his revenge, and it came together on November 14, 1963. Mobster Chuckie Grimaldi was there. When he rolled in 1972 and became a government witness, he provided prosecutors with his account of what happened that day.

He said that Sam's brother Mario tricked Foreman into

believing Sam was ready to let bygones be bygones, if Foreman helped fence a stolen diamond and paid back his debt. On November 14, 1963, Foreman was feeling such a sense of false security that he was playing cards with DeStefano in Sam's home. Shortly thereafter, Mario and Grimaldi arrived and they all left for Mario's house. When they arrived, Mario got Foreman to go down to his basement under the pretense of seeing his new bomb shelter. Once there, Mario and Grimaldi pulled guns and fired. Then Tony Spilotro, who was hiding in the basement, stepped out and fired. Foreman was lying on the floor, writhing in pain, but still alive.

At that point Mad Sam appeared, dressed in pajamas, and went right over to Foreman. Grabbing Foreman's face he cursed at him and told him he was going to be a blood sacrifice to Satan. After being viciously tortured, Foreman mercifully died. As DeStefano turned to leave, he looked down at the body and said, "Look. He's got a smile on his face. Looks like he was glad to die." He undoubtedly was. His body was stuffed into the trunk of a car that was left abandoned.

Mad Sam, Mario, Grimaldi, and Tony must have thought they were in the clear, but when Foreman's body was found a few days later, evidence technicians vacuumed his clothing and discovered paint and wood chips embedded in the fabric and sealed them as evidence. Seven years later, Mario sold his house. Investigators went in and were able to match the paint and wood chips they had saved since 1963 to similar material found in the basement, as well as blood specks.

With that physical evidence and Grimaldi then a government witness, Sam, Mario, and Tony were indicted for Foreman's murder.

Tony was in a tough spot, and it got worse when Sam announced he was going to represent himself in court. Tony and Mario didn't want any part of being in the courtroom with Sam and petitioned for separate trials. They were successful, and their trial was scheduled to start on April 30, 1973. That led to another murder I'll discuss shortly.

* * *

Manny Skar

In 1965, Mandel "Manny" Skar was forty-two years old, an ex-con who associated with a lot of Outfit guys. Skar was kind of a big mouth and liked to brag about his Mob connections. He was involved in the construction business and was also the owner of the Sahara Inn in Schiller Park from 1962 to 1963, when he sold it to cowboy star Gene Autry after falling behind on his payments. During the short time he had the place he was investigated by state and local agencies concerning his finances.

Skar's troubles with the law continued when the feds started breathing down his neck, claiming he'd evaded paying over a million dollars in taxes. When that happened the Outfit came to see him as a threat.

On September 11, the *Chicago Tribune* reported that Skar was shot and killed by unknown gunmen who ambushed him as he entered the parking garage of his apartment building at 3800 North Lake Shore Drive at around 12:40 a.m. Witnesses told the cops three men did the shooting and then fled the scene by car.

In a follow-up piece two days later, they said they had received information from unnamed sources that Skar was on the verge of making a deal to provide prosecutors with information about the Outfit's financial operations, in return for a break in his income tax case. They concluded Skar's death was most likely the result of a Mob hit.

The newspaper had most of it right, but here's a couple of things they didn't know. Skar had borrowed money from the Outfit for his Sahara Inn project and wasn't paying it back. That was bad, but the Outfit would have let him live because as long as he was alive, there was at least a chance of getting their money back. When he got into the tax problems, though, everything changed. Skar had to go.

Dicky Gorman told me there were actually four guys in on the hit and he was one of them. The shooters were him, Tony, and Joey (he didn't say if it was Lombardo or Hansen). Saint was their driver.

After the killing there was a lot of speculation that Lombardo was responsible, and that was when he made his bones with the Outfit. But it never got past the speculation stage. Nobody was ever charged with Skar's killing, and it remains officially unsolved.

* * *

Alan Rosenberg

In 1963, Tony Spilotro's pal and rising Mob boss Felix "Milwaukee Phil" Alderisio was involved with four other guys in a big financial scam. His cohorts were Irwin "Pinky" Davis, Burton Wolcoff, Harris Jacobs, and Alan Rosenberg. These four guys went to Bettendorf, Iowa, and formed a company called the Harris Discount Center. They ordered merchandise that was subsequently shipped to Phil in Chicago, where he disposed of it. Davis, Wolcoff, Jacobs, and Rosenberg didn't pay their creditors and allowed the company to go bankrupt. In August 1966, the four men were convicted in federal court in Des Moines for mail fraud conspiracy and violating the federal bankruptcy statute. Each defendant drew prison sentences plus fines. Alderisio wasn't charged.

There was a problem, though. The Harris Discount Center wasn't the only scam Milwaukee Phil had been involved in with Davis and Rosenberg.

After I first heard that Tony knew Davis, I asked him about it. "What kind of fuckin' guy would call himself Pinky?"

Tony laughed. "He's all right. He's got a lot of

connections, and him and his Jew buddy—a guy named Rosenberg—have got a good thing going with Phil. They bid on boxcar loads of damaged goods—things that have already been paid for by insurance and written off as losses. When they get the stuff, they pass it on to Phil, and he sells everything on the cheap. They've even got a big warehouse to stash all the merchandise until it's sold. It's a real money maker, Frankie."

"It sounds like it."

"The only trouble is, Pinky and Rosenberg are a little shaky and could fuck everything up."

"What do ya mean, they're shaky?"

"The law's putting the heat on them. We don't know how solid they are."

I laughed. "Don't tell me you're gonna have to off that fuckin' Pinky."

Tony was serious. "Not Pinky. But the Jew will probably have to go. When he does, Pinky will get the message. He's got a funny name, but he's not stupid."

"You got somebody lined up for the job?"

"Me and the German [Frankie Schweihs] will do it."

I knew it was coming, so I wasn't surprised when Alan Rosenberg was murdered "gangland style" on St. Patrick's Day in 1967. Rosenberg was free on bond at the time while he appealed his conviction in the Harris Discount Center case. Milwaukee Phil had sent his message.

Sam 'Mad Sam' DeStefano

I told you earlier that the murder of Mad Sam's associate Leo Foreman in 1963 led to another killing. This one took place almost ten years later, and the victim was none other than Mad Sam, himself. I never liked the guy and shed no tears when I learned he'd been whacked.

I first met Sam DeStefano in the early 1960s when Tony and I were sitting at the bar in the North Avenue Steak House. Sam came over, and Tony introduced us. He must have been drunk, because he was ranting and raving about future Outfit underboss Jackie Cerone and picking on everybody in the place. He was the obnoxious bully I figured he'd be based on what I'd heard about him. His reputation was that he didn't hesitate to take out anybody he thought had crossed him, but he didn't just kill, he tortured his victims and made sure they died slow. And it was common knowledge on the street that Sam killed his own younger brother Michael on the orders of Sam Giancana. That aside, he made a lot of money for the Outfit, and they tolerated his bullshit.

I didn't want anything to do with Mad Sam, but Tony and Dicky Gorman ended up doing collection work for him.

Like so many other mobsters and Mob associates, Sam became expendable when he was thought to be a threat to the organization. And that happened in April 1973, just a couple of weeks before the murder trials of Tony and Mario DeStefano and Mad Sam (who was being tried separately) in the Leo Foreman case were scheduled to start.

Tony and Mario had a reason to be worried. Not only was Sam going to represent himself, he'd been diagnosed with terminal cancer and the word was that he might be willing to make a deal with prosecutors to be allowed to die at home. They knew that any deal would require Sam to give them up and testify against them. Based on the fact that Sam had been willing to murder his sibling, there was no reason to think he wouldn't turn on them. There was only one thing to do.

On April 15, Sam was outside in his garage when he was killed by two blasts from a shotgun.

I was serving a sentence in Stateville Prison when I heard about the hit. I didn't know for sure who pulled the trigger, but there was no doubt in my mind it had something to do with the upcoming Foreman trial.

When I got out of prison in 1974, Tony was living in Vegas so I didn't get to see him very often. But a year or so later he was in Chicago and stopped at the disco I'd opened there. We talked for a long time, and Mad Sam's murder came up.

"Mad Sam was goin' fuckin' mad," Tony laughed. "Nobody knew what he was gonna do. There was a good chance he was gonna put me and Mario behind bars—and maybe some other people, too. We couldn't risk it."

Tony didn't say who gave the go ahead for the killing, but Joey Aiuppa was the boss at that time and he'd had to have given his approval. And then Tony told me how it went down.

"Mario and me told Sam we'd be over to talk about that fuckin' rat, Chuckie Grimaldi. We drove to Sam's in our work car [a fictitiously licensed vehicle]. Mario walked up the driveway ahead of me, and when we got close to Sam he stepped aside. I had the shotgun and let Sam have both barrels. He was dead before he hit the ground.

"We got the hell out of there and met up with Saint [driving the 'ram' car that would be used to break up any police pursuit] a few blocks away. We ditched the work car and took off with Saint. Problem solved."

Mad Sam's student had learned his lessons well.

A few weeks after Sam's death Tony was acquitted at trial in the Foreman case. One of the main reasons he got off was because of his alibi. A furniture store owner named Al Bruno testified that Tony was shopping in his store at Grand and Austin avenues in Chicago at the time Foreman was killed.

Interestingly, Bruno was married to the widow of Jimmy Miraglia—one of the guys Tony killed in 1962 as part of the M&M Murders—and was a friend of ours. He sure came through for Tony that time.

* * *

William 'Red' Klim

This is a killing that I have no knowledge of. I was in prison at the time, and Tony never mentioned it to me. I include it because it took place in Las Vegas where Tony was living, had elements that made him a logical suspect, and he was arrested for the murder.

On June 23, 1973, Klim, a Caesars Palace employee, was shot and killed gangland style in the parking lot of the Churchill Downs Race Book. According to reports, there were multiple theories regarding the motive for Klim's murder. One was that he was cooperating with authorities in an investigation of illegal bookmaking that targeted Outfit associate Lefty Rosenthal. Another suggested that Klim had information pertaining to Spilotro's implication in a federal fraud investigation underway in Chicago (see the Dan Seifert murder ahead) involving the Teamsters Pension Fund. Yet another designated Klim as a loan shark who refused to pay Tony a tribute. In each theory, Tony was tied in directly or as Rosenthal's protector. The case against Tony collapsed when witnesses couldn't or wouldn't positively identify the killer.

Whatever was going on with Klim, each of the scenarios would have resulted in a death sentence, and Tony is the guy who would have done it personally or had it done.

* * *

James Leonetti

In July 1973, a thirty-three-year-old man named James "Jimmy" Leonetti was shot to death inside Bill's Grill on West North Avenue in Melrose Park, Illinois, by two masked men. Jimmy's murder remains unsolved. Tony Spilotro didn't kill Jimmy or even order his murder, but he did give his approval to a plot that lured Jimmy to the murder site.

I know the background on Jimmy's killing because before I went to prison in 1969, I was stealing with him. He was a real tough kid, and I liked him. One day we were in the Colony House when Tony Spilotro came in. He saw us and nodded, then made a call on the payphone. After the call he came over to us and asked us to go for a ride with him.

We drove to Melrose Park, and Tony pulled up in front of a pool room and went inside. In a few minutes he came out with a thief named Sam Urbana and an Outfit guy named Louis "Louie the Mooch" Eboli. They stood in the doorway talking, and then the three of them walked over to Tony's car. Tony got in behind the wheel, I was in the passenger seat, and Jimmy was in the back. It was a warm night, and the car windows were down.

Eboli reached through the back window, grabbed Jimmy by the collar, and pulled him out of the car through the window. I said to Tony, "What the fuck's going on?"

"Just relax and don't get involved."

Louie threw Jimmy down and got on top of him, throwing punches. I figured Jimmy could take Louie any time he wanted, but he was just blocking the punches and not fighting back.

After a couple of minutes I said to Tony, "If Louie doesn't stop, I'll get out and stop it."

Tony nodded and hollered to Louie, "Are you satisfied?"

"Yeah," Louie said.

He got up, and he and Urbana went back inside. Jimmy got into the car.

Tony dropped Jimmy and me off at the Colony House. I said to Jimmy, "I feel bad about this. I don't want you to think I set you up."

"I know you didn't, it's got nothing to do with you. You know Louie supplies the jukeboxes and pinball machines to all the joints in the suburbs, right?"

"Sure, I know that."

"Well I made a special pick that opens the coin boxes on those machines, and I've been robbing them. Louie found out it was me and warned me to stop. I didn't, and he sent out the word that he was looking for me and this time I was gonna get a beating. If Tony didn't turn me over somebody else would have. That's why I didn't kick his ass and let him get it out of his system."

"What the hell's the matter with you? You've gotta stop that shit, or you'll get more than a beating."

"I know, I know," he said.

I went to prison shortly after that, and in July of 1973 I heard on the news that Jimmy had been whacked while he was in a joint in Melrose Park, supposedly waiting to meet someone who never showed up. *Don't tell me he was still robbing from those fucking machines!*

When I was released the following year and got back to Chicago, one of the things I was interested in finding out was why Jimmy got killed.

I stopped into Hoagies, the restaurant Michael Spilotro owned. He was quite excited to see me. We talked for a while, and then he pulled me aside and said, "You heard about Jimmy Leonetti?"

"Yeah, what the fuck is up with that?"

Michael shook his head sadly. "He started robbing Louie's machines again, and Louie was really pissed off. He said he'd given him all the warnings he was gonna get and asked me to help him set Jimmy up. I told him I needed to check with Tony first. I called Tony, and he said, 'Go ahead and set him up.' So I told Jimmy I'd meet him at Bill's that night and try to straighten things out between him and Louie."

When I saw Tony later I talked with him about it. "Jimmy was a good guy, Tony. Killing him was bullshit."

"I liked him, too, Frankie. But he was a stubborn bastard and wouldn't stay away from Louie's machines. Louie kicks up a lot of money to the Outfit, so it had to be done."

I didn't ask who did the hit, and Tony didn't say. My guess, though, is that Louie was behind it and may have been one of the shooters. The other two likely guys were Butch Petrocelli and Harry Aleman.

When I ran into a guy who had been close to Jimmy, he said Jimmy knew he was in trouble and might get killed. Jimmy told his friend, "If they get me, I want to be put in the casket on my stomach, so as those bastards walk by they can kiss my ass."

That was Jimmy.

* * *

Richard Scalzetti Cain

Richard Cain had a very interesting history. At one time he was a cop. Some called him the most corrupt cop in Chicago history because he was also a hit man for the Outfit. In addition, at various times he worked as an investigator for U.S. Attorney Richard Ogilvie and trained Cuban exiles prior to the Bay of Pigs invasion (possibly as a CIA contract agent). It was rumored he was an FBI informant and that he was the man who actually shot President Kennedy, not Lee Harvey Oswald. I knew Cain because of his involvement with the Outfit. He was a close associate of Sam Giancana and served as Sam's driver and bodyguard.

I met him twice. The first time was in 1963 after some guys robbed the Franklin Park (Illinois) Bank. I lived in Franklin Park at the time, and my house was less than a mile from the bank. The thieves asked if they could drop the money at my place right after the robbery. That way they'd be clean if the cops stopped them, and in return I'd get a cut of the take. They'd pick the money up a few days later after the heat was off. It sounded like easy money so I said okay.

They ran into some bad luck during the escape, though, when a train blocked their route and they had to jump out of their work cars and run for it. The three guys who had the money with them said they hid it between two houses where it wouldn't be noticed, and they'd pick it up in a couple of days. When they went back to get the money, it was gone.

The Outfit knew about the robbery and put the word out they wanted their tribute. They didn't believe the story that the money had disappeared. Each of the guys involved with the robbery in any way, including me, had to take a polygraph exam in order to convince the Outfit we were being truthful. The polygraphs were done in the back room of a restaurant owned by Mario DeStefano, Mad Sam's brother. The tests were given under the direction of Richard Cain. One of the guys failed the exam. His name was Guy Mendola, and not long afterward he was murdered—shotgunned in his driveway. Who did it, I don't know.

The next time I saw Cain was in the late 1960s or early '70s. I was temporarily transferred from Stateville Prison to the Cook County Jail while some cases I had pending went through the court system. Cain was housed there at the same time. I don't recall what charges he was on, but I'll always remember he wore a blue bathrobe and seldom took a shower. We used to tease him about not showering, and by the time I went back to Stateville he was spending a lot more time in the shower room.

In late December 1973, while I was locked up in the federal prison in Terre Haute, the story broke that Cain was murdered in Chicago on December 20 in Rosie's Sandwich Shop at 1117 West Grand Avenue. Reports were that three masked gunmen entered Rosie's and shot him twice in the head with a shotgun at close range, virtually decapitating him. Newspaper accounts said the restaurant was a favorite hangout for Outfit big shot Marshall Caifano, and Caifano had been at Rosie's for a time prior to the shooting. There was also speculation as to why Cain was hit. Theories ranged from Cain being suspected of being a snitch to a major falling out between him and Giancana over finances. I also read or heard—I don't remember which—that two of the gunmen were short in stature. That made me immediately think of Tony.

During one of the many conversations I had with Tony after I got out of prison in 1974, Cain's murder came up. Tony said, "You were in jail with him weren't you?"

"Yeah, we were in Cook County together for a while. Why?"

"What did that jackoff have to say?"

"Not much, Tony. He was a real quiet guy, but I knew he was tight with Giancana and Willie Potatoes [Outfit big shot William Daddano]. I had a connection with the deputy warden and got him to give Cain extra visits with his wife, and we teased him about the bathrobe he always wore. Other than that, I don't remember much about him."

Tony laughed. "Me, the Little Guy, and the German [Frankie Schweihs] whacked him."

I was surprised he said it like that, kind of a boast. It made sense, though. As I said, Tony came to my mind as one of the hitters as soon as I heard about the murder. I assumed the "Little Guy" Tony mentioned was Saint. He and Tony did a lot of things together, and Saint was the only guy Tony worked with who was shorter than he was.

Was Tony just blowing smoke that day for some reason? My money is on he was telling the truth.

* * *

Dan Seifert

Dan Seifert, age twenty-nine, owned a fiberglass molding company called Plastic-Matic Products in the Chicago suburb of Bensenville. In May 2009, the *Chicago Magazine* reported that on September 27, 1974, Seifert, his wife, Emma, and their four-year-old son stopped at the plant. They were in the office when the door burst open and two men dressed in hooded sweatshirts, ski masks, and carrying handguns came in.

According to Emma's account of the incident, her husband was clubbed in the head with the butt of a pistol and knocked down. And then she and the boy were shoved into the bathroom. After hearing a gunshot, Emma left the bathroom. She saw blood on the office wall but no sign of her husband or the gunmen. She opened the front door and saw Dan, wounded and running across the parking lot. Suddenly, a man with a shotgun materialized from behind a parked car and fired. Dan Seifert was dead.

I wasn't at the scene, but that *Chicago Magazine* article matches what I heard about how the hit went down. It also explains a motive for the killing, which I believe is 100 percent accurate.

A few years earlier, Dan Seifert entered into a business arrangement to open International Fiberglass. One of his associates was none other than "Milwaukee Phil" Alderisio. Not long after the business opened, friends of Phil's started stopping in or hanging around. They included Tony Spilotro, Frankie Schweihs, and Joe Lombardo.

By 1973 Seifert wanted to sever his relationship with them. He sold his interest in International Fiberglass and opened Plastic-Matic. Around the same time, the FBI approached him seeking his cooperation in their investigation of a large fraud involving a Teamster Pension Fund. They thought International Fiberglass may have been used to launder the money. Seifert agreed to help.

In 1974 six defendants were charged with defrauding the Central States Teamsters Pension Fund of $1.4 million. Among them were Tony Spilotro, Joe Lombardo, and Allen Dorfman, who was known to arrange financial transactions between the Teamsters and organized crime and had been convicted in a Teamster kickback case a few years earlier.

The government's scenario was complicated, with a lot of bookkeeping records that would have to be explained to a jury. Dan Seifert was going to be the man to walk the jurors through the maze of transactions in a manner they would be able to understand. He was the key witness.

Although Tony never admitted it to me, there was absolutely no doubt in my mind that he and Joey Hansen were two of the men who were at Dan Seifert's business that day. I believe there were two other guys with them. One would have been their driver, undoubtedly Saint. The other was likely from Arizona. I'm sure Joe Lombardo was at least a co-conspirator in the killing, but I'm not convinced he was actually at the scene.

I got confirmation years later that Tony was in on Seifert's murder from Joey Hansen, himself. Joey was living in California, and I ran into him there. During our conversation we talked about the old days and he said, "Back in the early '70s, Tony asked me if I'd help him whack a guy in Chicago who ran a fiberglass business and was causing problems. Tony, the guy from Arizona, and me did the job, and Saint drove the ram car."

Joe Aiuppa would have approved the hit. It's kind of funny because there's a saying that a grand jury can indict a ham sandwich, and the first time I ever heard it was from Joe Lombardo. The joke around Chicago was that Aiuppa would give permission to whack a ham sandwich.

Not long after the murder, Tony was dropped from the case, and all five of the other defendants were acquitted.

In 2005 Lombardo was one of several mobsters indicted by the feds in what was called Operation Family Secrets. One of the charges against him was killing Dan Seifert. In 2007, a jury found him guilty of all charges, including the Seifert murder.

* * *

Marty Buccieri

This killing is similar to the previously discussed Klim murder, in that Buccieri was also a Caesars Palace employee and I have no personal knowledge of the hit. But he did have some connection to the Outfit as a distant relative of Outfit underboss Fiori "Fifi" Buccieri.

In addition, he reportedly had connections to most of the Vegas organized crime figures worth knowing and used those connections to facilitate the granting of a number of Teamster Pension Fund loans to Allen Glick, CEO of Argent, the Outfit-installed owner of the Stardust, Hacienda,

Fremont, and Marina casinos.

In the summer of 1975, law-enforcement got word that Buccieri had approached Glick and demanded a $30,000 "finder's fee" for his help in obtaining the loans. At one point he's said to have physically threatened Glick. The Argent boss then supposedly informed Lefty Rosenthal of the incident. A few days later, Buccieri was found shot to death. Although Tony was a suspect, he wasn't arrested or charged.

If the reports are accurate, based on what I know Tony's role in Vegas was, I think the killing was ordered by Chicago and Tony assigned it to Joey Hansen.

* * *

Jimmy 'The Weasel' Fratianno

This is a murder I believe Tony authorized and assigned to Joey Hansen—it never came off, though. Tony told me about it in late 1979 but didn't mention a specific date or year. My best guess is that it probably took place in the mid-1970s.

Jimmy Fratianno was in the Los Angeles Mob. He was a hitter, and when the boss, Dominic Brooklier, was doing a couple of years in prison in the '70s, he promoted Fratianno to be the acting boss. By the time Brooklier was released, he was convinced Fratianno not only wasn't going to give up the boss's position, he was also providing information to the feds. Without enough muscle himself to challenge Fratianno, Brooklier contacted his friends in the Outfit looking for assistance. Tony had recently taken over the Outfit's Vegas operations, and his territory extended into Los Angeles. He was ordered to work with Brooklier to solve the Fratianno problem. However, Fratianno ended up becoming a government witness and went into the witness protection program in 1977. He was very effective in that capacity.

After I moved to Vegas, Tony and I were talking, and I

asked him about Fratianno.

Tony said, "That rat bastard. We knew he was talkin' to the G. I put Joey [Hansen] on him, but he was never able to get close to him. And then he went into the [Witness Protection] Program and was surrounded by marshals all the time. Now the prick's puttin' a lot of guys away."

Fratianno later said he became a government witness only after he learned Tony and Brooklier had put a contract on him.

Knowing what I know, I have no reason to doubt that Tony authorized Fratianno's murder and gave the job to Joey. It all adds up.

* * *

Sam Giancana

Former Outfit boss Sam Giancana was gunned down in the basement of his Oak Park home on June 19, 1975. It was reported that he was frying Italian sausage and peppers at the time and apparently let his killer in, leading investigators to believe it was someone he knew and trusted. Several names surfaced as suspects, including Tony Spilotro. I agreed that the killer was someone close to Sam, but I doubted very much it was Tony.

In the late summer of 1975 Tony came into Chicago from Vegas and stopped to see me. We talked about Giancana, and I asked Tony outright, "Did you whack him?"

Tony shook his head. "It wasn't me; it was [Dominic] Butch Blasi."

I knew Blasi was a long-time friend of Giancana and was surprised that he would have done the hit. I said, "Blasi? I thought him and Sam were tight."

"They were. Sam needed to go, and Butch was the only guy who could get close enough to him to do the job—that was that."

We then speculated on who would replace Giancana.

Tony said, "I'm trying to find out and should know soon."

A couple of days later he stopped back with the news. He said, "I'd been hoping this wouldn't happen, but it did."

"What are you talking about?"

"Jackie Cerone is going to take over for Sam. He's a fucking maniac, and that takes a lot of power away from me. I thought maybe they'd pick Turk [Torello], and I wish the fuck they had."

When Cerone was promoted he put Joe Lombardo in the second spot, and when Turk died in 1979 Lombardo replaced him as Tony's boss.

* * *

Louis M. Bombacino

Here's the background on Lou Bombacino. He was a Chicago bookie who hung with Outfit boss Jackie Cerone and the Elmwood Park crew. The FBI, looking to catch bigger fish, knew that Cerone had sided against Lou in a Mob dispute, so when Lou was in jail on robbery charges in June 1965 they approached him with an offer. They'd arrange for him to get off with a sentence of only probation if he'd go to work for them as an informant. Lou accepted.

As soon as he got released from jail, Lou resumed his role as a Mob bookie while secretly gathering evidence for the feds. In 1967, after two years of undercover work, the feds felt they had enough information to indict and convict several top mobsters and pulled Lou off the street. He was placed into the Witness Protection Program with the new name of Joseph Nardi, and he and his wife were relocated to Buckeye, Arizona, near Phoenix.

In 1969, the evidence Lou produced resulted in federal indictments against Cerone and four other major Outfit bigshots: Fiori "Fifi" Buccieri, Joe Ferriola, Donald Angelini, and Dominic Cortina. A couple of lesser players, James Cerone and Frank Aureli, were also charged. Lou

Bombacino testified at their trial, and all the defendants were subsequently convicted.

On the morning of October 6, 1975, Lou backed his car out of its parking space at his apartment building in Tempe, Arizona. Suddenly, a bomb planted in the car detonated with a thunderous explosion. Lou was killed instantly. Pieces of his car were found up to a quarter mile away and about a hundred windows in the apartment complex were shattered. An FBI spokesman called the bombing a "professional job." Their investigation determined that military grade plastique explosive had been used, and the bomb was triggered by wiring attached to the accelerator or steering wheel.

Although the killing was a suspected Mob hit, no one was charged with Lou's murder.

Now, here's what I know. After I got out of prison 1974, I went to Vegas every so often to see Tony and have a little fun. From there I'd drive to Los Angeles where I'd meet Joey Hansen, and we'd party for a couple of days.

On one of those trips—it would have been in 1977 or '78—when I saw Joey I kidded him about his thinning hair and how gray he was getting. He laughed and then said, "You've rigged [blown up] a car before, haven't you, Frankie?"

"Yeah, once. I blew up the car of a barber who was causing union problems. The barber and the roof of the car went about a hundred feet in the air. What about it?"

"Nerve-racking, isn't it?"

It was my turn to laugh. "Working with explosives can be a little stressful. You've done one?"

"Yeah, Tony and me got Lou Bombacino. Remember him?"

"Sure. That was you and Tony?"

Joey nodded. "Ronnie [DeAngelo] made a bomb for us that we could trigger with a remote. We rigged the car, and everything worked just like Ronnie said it would. I was afraid we'd blow ourselves up instead of Lou. I think that's why I've got so much gray hair," he added with a chuckle.

I hadn't thought about Tony doing that job when I first heard about it—I figured the Outfit had sent somebody from Chicago. After talking with Joey it made sense, though. Arizona was part of Tony's territory and Tony wasn't under constant surveillance back then, so he could move about pretty freely.

This is the only bombing Tony was connected to that I'm aware of.

* * *

Tamara Rand

One of the more memorable scenes in the movie *Casino* showed Joe Pesci killing a woman who was suing the owner of the fictional Tangiers Casino, and if the case moved forward it might have revealed hidden Mob control. That was based on the real-life Tamara Rand.

Tamara Rand was a friend and business partner of the previously mentioned Allen Glick. She invested heavily in his Vegas casinos, and in spite of having no gaming experience, had signed a contract as a consultant at the Hacienda for $100,000 per year. Rand believed that through those investments she had purchased 5 percent of Glick's casinos, so when Glick denied such a deal, she filed suit against him for breach of contract and fraud. A court trial could have blown the lid off the mob's hidden interests in the Las Vegas casinos. Consequently, on November 9, 1975, just days after a bitter argument between her and Glick, Tamara Rand was murdered at her home in San Diego. The murder weapon was a .22, believed by investigators to be Tony's weapon of choice.

According to reports, Tony was a prime suspect in the murder, but there was insufficient evidence to charge him with the crime.

Here's the story on the Rand murder. I got out of prison in 1974 and was living in Chicago. Several months after my release, Tony was in town from Vegas and we got together, as we always did when he was in on business. On this occasion he asked me when I was gonna move to Vegas to give him a hand. I told him I couldn't because I was still on parole. Then he asked if I was up for whacking a broad. He said the hit would be in California and asked if I could sneak out there and take care of it for him. I explained that my parole officer stopped by my place unannounced. I couldn't take a chance on disappearing for a couple of days and ending up back in the slammer. Tony said he understood, and that was the end of it until I moved to Vegas in 1979.

One day when Tony and I were talking I mentioned the Rand killing. "Was she the broad you talked to me about that time in Chicago?"

"Yeah. I got Joey in California to handle it for me. He took another guy with him and got it done."

I knew "Joey" was Joey Hansen. Although he didn't identify the second guy, Los Angeles mobster Frank "Bomp" Bompensiero is often mentioned as having been involved. Tony was friends with Bompensiero, so that's a possibility.

And if you're wondering why Tony wasn't doing many hits personally any more, remember that he had gotten too high profile by the mid-1970s. The cops and feds were watching him, making it almost impossible to do things himself. And he knew he'd be a suspect in the death of anybody that was a threat to him or the Outfit. By using other people he could establish solid alibis for himself and avoid being arrested or charged.

* * *

Ned Bakes, Frank DeLegge Jr. & Chuckie Nicoletti

Frank DeLegge was the nephew of Willie "Potatoes" Daddano. He was also an Outfit associate, thief, and killer.

He often worked with his father, and both were part of the crew that pulled the botched bank robbery in Franklin Park in September of 1963.

Frank had a beef with a Jew named Ned Bakes over something or other and wanted to whack him. I met Bakes when I was in prison. He was a schemer and hustler who made a lot of money for the Outfit, and more importantly, he was tight with Tony Accardo.

When Frank asked Chuckie Nicoletti (one of the bosses) for permission to kill Bakes, Chuckie took it to two of his peers as required, and the request was denied. For some unknown reason, Chuckie gave Frank the go-ahead anyway. On December 3, 1975, Frank and his partner, Gerri Scarpelli, put a bullet in Bakes's head and stuffed his body into the trunk of his car.

Accardo and the other Outfit bosses weren't happy. Scarpelli was questioned and said Frank had told him the hit had been approved by Nicoletti. Because Scarpelli hadn't knowingly violated Mob protocol he was given a pass, provided he help set Frank up to be killed. He agreed.

On November 20, 1976, Scarpelli lured Frank into his car to drive to a fake business meeting. In the backseat was Louie the Mooch Eboli, who later participated in the murders of Tony Spilotro and his brother Michael.

As they were riding, Eboli slipped a garrote over Frank's head and strangled him. Thinking he was dead, they threw him out on the side of the road. An autopsy showed that Frank didn't die of the strangulation. He actually bled to death from injuries he suffered when he was thrown out of the moving car.

There was a lot of speculation about who actually did the killing, and Tony's name was put out there. This is one he didn't do, but he knew who did.

Frank was gone, but Nicoletti still had to answer for what he'd done. It turned out that I was one of the last people to see him alive.

It was March 29, 1977, and I was in my lounge called Spanky's. Chuckie stopped in. He was having a drink at the bar, and I joined him. As we talked I could tell he was pretty down. He said he had a lot of headaches over something he'd done, but he thought it was the right thing. I didn't know what he was talking about, and he never said. Anyway, we bullshitted for about an hour, and then he said he had to go to the Golden Horns restaurant in Northlake.

An hour or so later I got a call from a friend. He said, "Did you hear what happened?"

"What do you mean?"

"They just whacked Chuckie Nicoletti in his car in the parking lot of the Golden Horns."

I couldn't believe it. "He was just in my joint. I talked with him for over an hour."

"That might be, but he's dead now."

When I hung up the phone I got to thinking that whoever whacked Chuckie might have been watching him while he was in my place and tailed him to the restaurant where they did the hit. But Chuckie was a big shot who'd eliminated a lot of problems for the Outfit, so I couldn't understand why they killed him.

It was later that I found out about the Ned Bakes thing directly from Tony. I was teasing him and said I'd seen his name in the papers as a possible suspect in the DeLegge killing.

He laughed. "Whenever anybody gets whacked my name comes up—it's automatic. You know that."

"So you didn't kill the guy?"

"No. Gerry Scarpelli and Louie the Mooch did it."

Then he gave me the whole story about Bakes and DeLegge, and how Chuckie Nicoletti had screwed up and had to go, too. After hearing that, it all fell into place.

I said, "Yeah, Chuckie really fucked up, didn't he? He was in my joint just before he went to the restaurant. He told me he was having some problems."

"You've gotta follow the rules, Frankie. Chuckie found that out the hard way. Butch [Petrocelli] and Harry [Aleman] got him in the parking lot before he had a chance to get out of his car."

Butch may have helped the Outfit deal with a problem, but it didn't endear him to them. They hit Butch a couple of months after the Nicoletti hit. Harry died in prison of natural causes in 2010.

The murders of Bakes, DeLegge, and Nicoletti are all officially unsolved.

* * *

Rick Manzie

Rick Manzie was married to black singer and actress Barbara McNair. McNair died on February 4, 2007. Two days later an article by Ed Koch ran in the *Las Vegas Sun* to talk about McNair, her life, and her career. It said in part:

"Las Vegas entertainer Barbara McNair was all smiles on Dec. 14, 1976, as she performed at Chicago's Condesa del Mar nightclub.

"Her mother-in-law, Pearl Manzie, had flown in from Las Vegas for the opening-night show and surprised her with news that McNair's husband/manager, Rick Manzie, planned to join them that weekend."

From Koch's piece it certainly seemed that McNair had reason to smile that night. But things changed very quickly for her. Around 7:00 a.m. the next day she received word that her husband of nearly four years was dead. And he hadn't died of an accident or natural causes. He'd been shot multiple times in the back of his head in the couple's Las Vegas home.

Koch mentioned Manzie's alleged ties to some reputed organized crime figures but stopped short of speculating on who the killer was.

Here's what the reporter didn't know. After I moved to

Vegas a friend told me that Tony was dating Barbara McNair. He'd been involved with her for a while, but since Manzie's death he said Tony was kind of "managing" her, making sure she got good bookings.

In the same conversation that we talked about Tamara Rand, I asked Tony about McNair. "I hear you're dating that black singer McNair."

He laughed. "That's right. I've been nailing her."

I smiled. "She's a widow, too."

"She was married to a real piece of shit. He was a fuckin' coke addict and used to punch her around a lot. I told him more than once to keep his hands off her, but he didn't."

"I know he got whacked."

Tony laughed again. "Joey [Hansen] and our friend from Arizona came in and took care of that little bastard for me."

Chalk another one up to the Little Guy.

* * *

The Manzie killing brings us up to my joining Tony again in Las Vegas. We've covered a lot of killings already, and we aren't quite done yet. However, you'll notice that as the FBI and Vegas cops put the heat on us, Tony began planning more murders than actually got done.

Barbara McNair and husband Rick Manzie. Manzie was murdered in 1976 on the orders of Tony Spilotro (courtesy Las Vegas News Bureau).

Thief and killer Richard "Dicky" Gorman circa early 1960s. He was considered to be a "sleeper" because he had no criminal record.

Frank "Lefty" Rosenthal (left) and killer Joey Hansen circa mid-1960s. (courtesy of Ross Stanger)

Tony Spiotro (second from left) and killer Paul Schiro (far right) circa early 1970s.

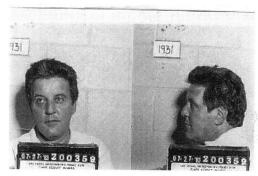

Tony's mug shots

*Las Vegas Metro
Lt. Gene Smith*

*Las Vegas Sheriff John
McCarthy 1979*

*The Hole in the Wall Gang following their arrest at Bertha's on
July 4, 1981. From left, Ernie Davino, Larry Neumann, Wayne
Matecki, Leo Guardino, Joe Blasko and Frank Cullotta*

Allen R. Glick served as the strawman for the Mob's hidden ownership and control of several Las Vegas casinos. He did business as the Argent Corporation. Courtesy UNLV Library

Former Cleveland mobster Moe Dalitz. Courtesy UNLV Library

Tony (left) & his attorney Oscar Goodman on their way to court in Las Vegas. Courtesy UNLV Library

Lefty Rosenthal (seated at left) on the set of his TV show at the Stardust. Courtesy UNLV Library

FBI agent Charlie Parsons

*This building housed Bertha's Gifts &
Home Furnishings on July 4, 1981*

Frank Cullotta

*FBI agent Dennis
Arnoldy, Las Vegas
case agent for the Tony
Spilotro investigations*

FBI agent Emmett Michaels

Larry Neumann's 2004 prison photo. Courtesy Illinois Department of Corrections

Las Vegas Mayor Oscar Goodman (publicity photo)

A handcuffed Tony Spilotro escorted by FBI agents (from left) Mark Kaspar, Dennis Arnoldy & Charlie Parsons

Michael Spilotro

Sherwin "Jerry" Lisner's mug shot. Lisner was murdered by Frank Cullotta in 1979

Outfit boss Joey Lombardo

Outfit associate Sam "Mad Sam" DeStefano

PART TWO

Las Vegas

12

THE SKIM

I'm opening this section talking about the skim because in order to fully appreciate what the Outfit had at stake in Las Vegas—what Tony was tasked with protecting—you have to understand the skim. Some examples of the skim were shown in the movie *Casino*, but the film didn't go into the background of it or the details of how it worked. The skim was what Vegas was all about from the Outfit's perspective. Although the other stuff Tony got into there— loan sharking, burglaries, robberies, arson, and other street crimes—put some money into the pockets of the Outfit bosses, Chicago's priority was to keep the skim running smoothly. I find it kind of ironic that the guy the Outfit had so much confidence in ended up contributing to the Outfit's downfall in Vegas. In my opinion, Tony's greed and quest for power eventually united the FBI and Las Vegas Metro and brought on the heat that was largely responsible for bringing it all down.

I'll explain the skim in a way that's easy to understand and tell you who was involved.

The basic premise behind the skim was to remove large chunks of money from the casinos prior to it officially being entered into the books as revenue. That included cash taken in from table games and the coins from slot machines. Cash was removed directly from the count rooms in duffle bags. The coins were weighed, not counted, and the casinos simply adjusted the scales to allow the mobsters to get their cut. Taxes weren't paid on the skimmed money, and the casinos involved basically functioned as piggy banks for the Midwest crime bosses.

It was important to keep the skim running smoothly and quietly, and Tony Spilotro was sent to Vegas to make sure that happened. So if it weren't for the Mob's hidden ownership and control over the casinos and the need to protect the status quo, there may never have been a Tony Spilotro—or me—in Las Vegas.

* * *

Organized crime figures weren't allowed to own casinos. To get around that rule the bosses used a land developer from California with no criminal record named Allen R. Glick to be their front man. Under the name Argent Corporation, Glick received an initial loan of $62 million from the Teamster Central States Pension Fund to purchase four Las Vegas casinos—the Stardust, Fremont, Hacienda, and Marina. The loans were assured due to the crime families in Kansas City, Milwaukee, and Cleveland having control of the trustees who had to approve them. The Outfit became the fourth and dominant member of the alliance. Over the lifetime of Argent, Glick received a total of $146 million in Teamster money.

The bosses in Chicago at that time were Tony Accardo and Joey Aiuppa. Kansas City was run by Nick Civella, Milwaukee by Frank "Bal" Balistrieri, and Milton Rockman represented Cleveland.

The Stardust became Argent's headquarters, but although Glick was the owner of record, the real boss was Lefty Rosenthal. The skimming took place at the Stardust and Fremont.

Now that you have a better idea of what was going on in Vegas and how much the Outfit and other families lost, I'll move on to when I reunited with Tony in Sin City.

13

KING OF THE STRIP

When I got into Vegas in 1979 my first stop was at Tony's Gold Rush jewelry store on West Sahara. Tony and Herb "Fat Herbie" Blitzstein (Tony's friend and bookie from Chicago) were standing outside the store when I pulled up. Tony walked over to the car, and we talked for a few minutes, agreeing to meet for dinner around six o'clock.

Over dinner Tony told me what my duties were going to be. He wanted me to put together a crew of guys to watch his back and provide muscle as necessary. The guys couldn't be Outfit men or known to the local cops. They could know we were working for Tony, but they couldn't have any direct contact with him—they'd get their orders from me.

"Who are we gonna muscle?" I asked.

"There are a lot of freelance bookies out here that aren't kicking anything back to me. They've gotta be brought into line and start paying me a street tax or be put out of business. I'll let you know who they are. The same thing goes for drug dealers. You can shake them down and make them pay me a tribute or take their drugs and money and close them up. Who the fuck are they gonna complain to?"

I nodded. "What else?"

"Anybody who steals from us or our [Outfit-controlled] casinos will have to be dealt with. And we'll have to take care of anybody who tries to muscle in on our businesses. I might have special jobs for you to do sometimes, too. What do you say?"

"That's fine, but these guys I get aren't going to be getting regular paychecks. They're going to have to earn in order to survive—they'll have to steal."

"They can steal. I got the okay on that from Chicago. On big scores they'll have to kick up 10 or 20 percent, depending on the take. On small scores—say $5,000 or less—they can keep it all."

"Okay. Is that it?"

"For your crew, yeah, but I'm gonna need you to personally take care of some things that I can't do myself. You're going to have to handle stuff for me inside the casinos."

I knew Tony's name had been added to the Nevada Gaming Control Board's so-called Black Book in October 1978, because of his organized crime ties. Having been declared an undesirable, he was banned from all casino properties. "What will I have to do?"

"You've got to be my eyes and ears. If there are any problems you'll have to take care of them. And when people from Chicago come out, you'll have to make sure their rooms, food, beverages, and entertainment get comped. I'll give you the names of all the casino people you'll need to know, and you can introduce yourself."

"No problem."

"And you're going to have to keep your eye on the Jew [Lefty Rosenthal]. Even though he couldn't get a gaming license the arrogant bastard is still hanging around the Stardust, and I want to know what the fuck he's up to."

"I haven't seen him since 1961. Does he still look the same?"

"He looks the same. When you start going into the Stardust you'll see him and he'll see you. He'll keep away from you and won't even let on he knows you."

By the time we finished our dinner, it was obvious to me that Tony had built an impressive criminal empire in his eight years in Vegas and was intent on expanding it. He had his old Chicago buddies Paulie Schiro and Joey Hansen helping with his business interests in Arizona and Southern California. Early on Tony had also recruited a New York guy named Joey Cusumano to stay close to Lefty, who was then running the Stardust. It was a good move that kept Lefty from having direct contact with Outfit guys that could be used against him by the law or gaming regulators. Cusumano also functioned as a liaison between Tony and the New York mobsters operating in Vegas, a role that continued after Lefty was ousted from his position at the Stardust.

* * *

Before I continue I want to say a little more about Cusumano. Soon after I got into town Tony asked me to take a ride with him. He had a Corvette that was used as a pace car at the races and was worth a lot of money. He said he was going to see a friend of his from New York who ran a car rental business and see if he was interested in selling the Vette for him.

The guy was Joey Cusumano. Tony introduced us, and I didn't like him from the start. I thought he was pretty arrogant and didn't like the way he handled himself around Tony. Tony talked to him about the car, and then we left.

The next time I saw Cusumano was at My Place Lounge. A guy from a motorcycle gang (Hell's Angels or Outlaws) came in, took a seat at the bar, and told the bartender he wanted to see the Little Guy. Tony wasn't there so the bartender told me about it.

I went over to the guy and said, "What do you want to see Tony about?"

"I figure if he wants to partner with us we'd be able to do a lot of things in this town."

"I'll see if I can get hold of him."

I went to the pay phone, called Tony, and told him he should come and talk to the guy. I met Tony at the door, and he went right to the phone and called Cusumano. Tony said, "Come to My Place and bring your piece."

At this stage in our careers, Tony and I never carried a gun unless we planned to use it. In case the biker turned out to be trouble, Tony wanted a gun close by and Cusumano was going to provide it.

When Cusumano showed up he flashed a snub-nosed .38 and then took a place at the end of the bar. Tony and I stood on either side of the biker, and he and Tony talked. He went on and on about how his gang could come in and together we could take over the town.

When Tony had heard enough he told the guy he'd better leave while he was still in one piece and if he ever came back there'd be trouble. The biker left without an argument, and that was the last we saw of him.

I saw Cusumano with Tony again when Tony got shot. Tony and his girlfriend Mary were in the My Place, and she wanted to go home. Tony left to drive her. He was back in less than half an hour, and when he came in he was limping.

I said, "What happened to you?"

"I got shot."

"Shot?"

He pointed to his foot, and it was bloody.

Tony explained, "When we got to Mary's place and got out of the car, a young guy with a rifle tried to stick us up. He was shaking pretty bad, and I was afraid he might shoot one of us by accident. I got close enough to him to grab the barrel, and when I did the gun went off. The bullet got me in the foot.

"The kid was scared. He said he had no money and was desperate. He begged me not to kill him. I told him to beat it."

"Are you going to get that foot looked at?"

"Yeah, but I can't go to the hospital with a gunshot wound. I'll call Joey, and he'll get me to somebody."

Tony made the call, and Cusumano showed up a short time later. He took Tony to a veterinarian who was on juice, and the guy bandaged Tony up. The story never got out to the cops or the media.

My last dealing with Cusumano was when Tony and I were in the Upper Crust and I showed him some jewelry from a burglary. He was looking the stuff over when an expensive gold brooch caught his eye. He called Cusumano and told him to come over. He showed him the piece and said, "Do you recognize this?"

"Yeah, I do."

"That's what I thought."

What the fuck was this all about?

I asked, "Am I going to have to give this stuff back?"

Tony said, "No, you can keep it."

It turned out that Lefty Rosenthal had bought the piece from Tony and given it to one of the dancers at the Stardust. Because Cusumano was close with Lefty he was able to identify it.

It was clear that Tony and Cusumano had a relationship and Tony had confidence in him. On one occasion, though, I caught Cusumano in a lie involving a New York guy named Frank Citro.

I got a call from my lawyer, John Momot, that Citro wasn't happy with him and was threatening him. Momot was worried and asked if I could do anything to get Citro to leave him alone. I didn't know Citro personally, but his reputation was that he was a real tough guy and nobody to fool with. I called Tony and told him what was going on.

He said, "When Momot does work for us we don't want him thinking about anything else. I'll tell Joey [Cusumano] to get a message to Citro to let it go."

I thought that would be the end of it, but it wasn't. Momot called me a couple of weeks later and said things were getting worse with Citro. He again asked me to intervene. This time I went to a New York guy I knew who worked at the Hacienda. I said I needed to talk with Citro and asked him to see if Citro would meet me at my Upper Crust restaurant. The meeting took place a few days later.

When Citro arrived, we shook hands and I asked him to come into my office to talk. Very politely, I explained my relationship with Momot and that Tony and I would appreciate it if he'd drop his beef against him. I wasn't sure how he'd react and was ready for anything.

However, he was very calm and respectful. "No problem, Frankie, whatever the Little Guy wants I'll do. You can tell him and Momot I'll back off as of right now."

Before Citro left I asked him if Cusumano had talked with him about Momot. He said, "Cusumano? No, was he supposed to?"

I shrugged. "I guess not."

Afterward, I told Tony I had to talk with him. When we got together I asked. "Did you tell Cusumano about the Citro thing?"

"Yeah, he said he took care of it. Why?"

"He didn't. I talked with Citro myself, and everything's okay now—he's dropping it."

I thought Tony would be pissed off, but he just shook his head and let it drop.

Those were my dealings with Cusumano, and because Tony's management style was to keep things compartmentalized, I never did find out exactly how deeply Cusumano was involved.

* * *

Understandably, when Tony and I finished our talk that evening I was upbeat. It looked like I had the best of all worlds. I would be the crew boss, could steal at will, and would hold sway in the Outfit-connected casinos.

On the downside, there were a couple of things I didn't fully realize at the outset. One was that Tony's decision not to pay the crew I put together and instead let them steal for a living would have consequences. It unleashed a crime wave that resulted in tremendous heat from the local cops and the feds.

The other thing was that the FBI and Las Vegas Metro Police—who hadn't been getting along—had recently mended their fences and were working jointly. They already had made bringing Tony down their top priority.

* * *

Within a few days of that initial meeting I began to assemble my crew, which would become known as the Hole in the Wall Gang. The cast of characters changed from time to time, but the guys I'm going to mention were the nucleus. My first recruit came through another Chicago guy I knew who was living in Vegas, Joey DiFronzo, who was a thief and the brother of Outfit big shot Johnny "No Nose" DiFronzo. Joey introduced me to Ernie Davino. Ernie was from New Jersey—Hoboken I think—and worked as a masseuse at a place called the Sports Club. When Ernie knew a customer left a lot of cash or jewelry in his locker while working out, he'd call Joey who would come over and break into the locker and give Ernie a cut of the score. He was a short, muscular guy, and while he was primarily a thief, he wasn't afraid to play rough if he had to. I had my first recruit.

I next contacted Leo Guardino, another thief from Chicago who was living in Vegas. Leo was a few years older than me and was known as a master thief—a dedicated burglar. He was trying to go legit in Vegas and was having trouble landing a decent job. When I talked to him, he was ready to listen.

I said, "I'm working for Tony Spilotro, and I'm putting a crew together. You interested?"

"What's the setup?"

"We'll do our own scores and any that Tony tells us about. All we have to do is kick up some of the money from our jobs to Tony and fulfill our other obligations to him."

"What kind of obligations?"

"That depends. He'll probably want us to muscle people once in a while. Maybe shake down drug dealers and renegade bookies—things like that."

"I don't mind a little rough stuff, but I'm not a killer. I don't want to get into that kind of shit."

"Don't worry about it; you won't have to do anything you don't want to do. I'll have some other guys around to handle things like that."

"Tony's an Outfit guy. What about them? Where do they fit in?"

"Tony will determine how much money has to be sent to Chicago. We'll make a lot of money for ourselves, too; you can count on it. On top of that, we'll have carte blanche at some of the casinos. Shows, meals, and stuff will all be comped. I'm setting that up now. We'll be living the good life."

I had the second member of my crew, who also became my partner in the Upper Crust.

My next contact was Wayne Matecki, who had worked for me as a doorman when I ran a lounge in Chicago. Wayne looked more like a computer nerd than the thief and killer he was. He didn't want to move out of Chicago and wouldn't be a regular part of my crew, but I'd promised Leo Guardino I'd have guys available to handle the heavy work. Wayne agreed to work with me on killings or really big scores.

After getting Wayne onboard I had to go back to Chicago to wrap up some business. While I was there I got in touch with Larry Neumann, whom I met in Stateville Prison in Illinois in 1968. He was serving a 125-year sentence for three 1956 murders but had managed to get parole after only doing around twelve years and was back on the street. I told him about a jeweler I knew named Bob Brown. This Brown always had about $100,000 of jewelry in his place and would make a good score. I hooked him up with Wayne Matecki to give him a hand with the robbery. The plan was for Larry to bring the jewelry to me in Vegas, I'd fence it to a couple of Arabs I knew, and we'd split the take three ways. The only bad thing was that Allen Dorfman—the guy who arranged Teamster loans for the Outfit—was a friend of Brown's. That meant I couldn't tell Tony about the robbery.

Wayne and Larry did the job, and a couple of days later Larry showed up at my door in Vegas carrying an attaché case. I said, "It looks like everything went well."

Larry said, "We got the jewelry, but we had to change the plan a little."

"What do you mean?"

"I had to kill him."

"You killed Brown?"

"I didn't intend to when I got there. But it was in the back of my mind that the Outfit might figure out who did the robbery and come after us. When I got in the store I said 'fuck it.' I put my gun down and grabbed a machete that was hanging on the wall. I started stabbing him, and Wayne broke a vase over his head."

I couldn't believe a simple robbery had turned into a murder. But what was done was done. After I fenced the stuff we ended up with about $25,000 each. It was hardly worth anybody's life.

Although I wasn't happy about the killing, I asked Larry if he was interested in moving to Vegas and being part of my crew. He said there was nothing holding him in Chicago and stayed in Vegas.

I figured between Ernie Davino, Leo Guardino, Wayne Matecki, Larry Neumann, and me, we could handle any size score and do anything from stealing to arson and murder.

Like I said, there were other guys who stole with us on occasion, but the five of us were the core of the Hole in the Wall Gang.

14

A CLOSER LOOK

Before I continue with my role as Tony's street lieutenant in Las Vegas, I want to talk about a few of the players Tony was already involved with before I arrived on the scene. Some of them were well known and others not so much, but they were all a part of Tony's realm. I've already talked a little about Lefty Rosenthal, but I have more to say. I also want to give you a little background about a couple of other guys I'll talk about in the pages ahead, a disgraced federal judge and a retired bootlegger. Two of them were thought to be Tony's allies but, in my opinion, may have done him more harm than good.

Let's begin with Lefty Rosenthal. Although I believe Tony was partly responsible for the Outfit losing Las Vegas, he wasn't the only one to point a finger at. The Outfit bosses could have managed things better, and at a minimum, Lefty let his mouth and ego get the best of him.

As I mentioned earlier, Tony and Lefty weren't close friends. In fact, Tony came to despise him. In spite of that, they needed to have a working relationship in order to carry out their duties, and for a while they did. Then Tony screwed up bad by having an affair with Lefty's wife, and Lefty blew it when he got into a battle with the Gaming Commission over his attempt to get a gaming license for his position at the Stardust. Because of their fuckups, both of them eventually fell out of favor with the Mob—Tony outlived his usefulness to the Outfit and Lefty was literally on Kansas City boss Nick Civella's hit list. Here's some background.

In 1974 Lefty applied for a gaming work card in Las Vegas. Applicants who were key employees of a casino were subjected to rigorous background investigations, with their friends and associates receiving special scrutiny. Lefty's relationship to Tony Spilotro and the Chicago Outfit resulted in his application being denied. Represented by Oscar Goodman, Lefty appealed the decision and won when the courts determined the denial of his application had been too hasty and that he'd been deprived of his ability to hold a key casino position without prior notice or the opportunity to be heard.

Following Lefty's victory, the Nevada Legislature sprang into action and passed legislation mandating that anyone found to be unqualified for a gaming license couldn't be employed by or have any contact with a casino licensee, except as an entertainer. This exemption allowed stars such as Frank Sinatra, who were believed to have ties to organized crime, to perform in the casinos. Seeing a chance to sidestep the whole licensing issue, Lefty gave himself the non-gaming title of Entertainment Director.

To help justify that title he taped a weekly variety show at the Stardust that was broadcast by a local TV station on Saturday evenings. "The Frank Rosenthal Show" was considered by many to be horrible, but it drew an audience. Guests included such celebrities of the day as Frank Sinatra, O.J. Simpson, and Frankie Valli, along with a bookmaker or two.

What got Lefty in trouble with Civella was that he used the show to take shots at the Gaming Commission. None of the bosses liked the idea of Lefty drawing unnecessary attention to his licensing issues, but on top of that, Civella had heard that Lefty was getting friendly with some FBI agents and was afraid he might roll if the going got tough.

Gaming regulators and law enforcement weren't fooled by Lefty's title—they were sure he was actually running things and Allen Glick, the owner of record, was only a front man—so Lefty was again told that his duties required him to obtain a gaming license. The subsequent hearings over his status and eligibility to be licensed often got heated, and Lefty openly attacked the Gaming Commission and its chairman, future U.S. Senator Harry Reid.

An encounter between Lefty and Reid was dramatized in a scene in *Casino*, in which actor Dick Smothers played a character based on Reid. Although there was some Hollywood in that scene, Tony had told me that Reid was in fact viewed as an ally and did receive special treatment and comps at the Stardust. What Reid did in return for those comps I don't know, but I *do* know that with the Mob you don't get something for nothing. There is no doubt in my mind that Reid took some action or inaction that benefited the Outfit.

Anyway, the battle between Lefty and the Commission was a hot topic in Vegas and was widely reported in the newspapers and on TV, exactly what the crime families wanted to avoid. Mob protocol is that you don't air your dirty laundry in public—that's done in private. His inability to follow that protocol made Lefty a "dry snitch," someone who reveals things during public statements that can cause harm to the organization.

When his application for a license was denied, Lefty, like Marshal Caifano before him, compounded the problem by filing a lawsuit against the Commission and the commissioners individually, generating additional publicity. The suit was eventually dismissed, and Lefty's active role in running the Stardust was over.

In October 1982, a few months after I rolled, Lefty's car blew up when he left Tony Roma's restaurant on East Sahara. He survived with fairly minor injuries. There was a lot of speculation as to who planted the bomb. I'm pretty confident that Nick Civella was behind it. Remember, he'd been in favor of whacking Lefty for a long time and with the FBI's skimming investigations heating up, his concern that Lefty might cooperate or already be cooperating with the feds probably resurfaced. Civella's hunch was apparently right because Lefty was never charged with any crimes and his role as an informant has been confirmed by other sources. Yeah, I think the car bomb was because Nick Civella decided it was time for Lefty to go.

* * *

Another guy who is thought of as having done great things for Tony is lawyer Oscar Goodman. Tony met Oscar through Lefty Rosenthal. Tony explained to me that when he first moved to Vegas in 1971, Sheriff Ralph Lamb wanted to send him a message that Lamb ran the town and Tony had better not fuck with him. He got Tony's attention by arresting him on a trumped up murder charge and putting him in jail. Tony reached out to Lefty looking for legal help and got an introduction to Oscar. The charges were quickly dropped, but Tony got the message. He kept clear of Lamb and operated pretty free of local law enforcement until Lamb lost his reelection bid in 1978 and was replaced by John McCarthy.

Tony had great confidence in Oscar and used him as his legal representative right up until the end. And with all the things Tony was suspected of, he never was convicted of anything and didn't serve any time. Oscar did a hell of a job for Tony, right? It might look that way, but I see it different and here is why.

Oscar was a master at getting delays in cases Tony was charged in, but he very seldom got acquittals—the unresolved cases remained out there and would have to be settled someday. That put a lot of stress on Tony, and I'm sure it eventually affected his health and judgment. Some of the Chicago bosses even thought Tony was a prime candidate to switch sides as the pressure on him increased.

Before the Bertha's trial in 1986, Tony had a chance to make a deal with the feds that would have required some prison time but would have gotten him out of the eye of the storm alive. Tony and Oscar refused the government's offer, and soon after Tony was dead. It was a poor decision on both of their parts.

* * *

Harry Reid has been the subject of much speculation regarding his alleged association with the Mob. As I already said, according to Tony there was a relationship, I just don't know how deep it was.

However, Reid has been involved in some incidents that are a matter of public record. For example, in 1978 Reid claimed a man named Jack Gordon offered him a bribe of $12,000 to approve a gaming device that would have produced a handsome profit. Reid informed the FBI about the bribe offer and agreed to let them film a meeting between him and Gordon in Reid's office. According to published reports, when Reid asked Gordon about the bribe money, agents entered the room to arrest Gordon. At that point Reid shouted at Gordon, "You son of a bitch; you tried to bribe me!" He then attacked Gordon and tried to strangle him. Gordon was convicted and spent six months in prison.

On July 29, 1981, Reid reported that his wife's car had been sabotaged by someone running a cable from the battery to the gas tank in an attempt to cause an explosion. There was speculation that the device was the work of either Jack Gordon in an attempt to get revenge or Lefty Rosenthal in retaliation for his treatment by the Gaming Commission.

I can state with certainty that this thing—if it actually happened—was not the work of the Outfit on behalf of Lefty. To begin with, I hadn't rolled yet and would have been asked to do the job or at least heard about it. Second, the "bomb" was strictly amateur and no real hit man would have done it that way. Last but not least, if we wanted Reid dead we wouldn't have targeted a vehicle used primarily by his wife and kids. If the Outfit had wanted Reid dead he'd have been dead. You can take that to the bank.

How much of an asset Reid was to Tony will probably never be known, because Tony can't say and Reid won't say.

* * *

Next is Nevada federal district court Judge Harry Claiborne. If you're a mobster it pays to have friends in high places, and according to Tony, we had one in Claiborne. Tony said Claiborne was a good friend of Oscar Goodman, and if we had any federal cases and could get them in front of Claiborne, we'd have a good chance of coming out okay.

I was never a defendant in a case before Claiborne, so I can't cite personal experience. I have no reason to doubt what Tony told me, though, and believe Claiborne was in the Outfit's pocket. Add to that the fact that in 1983 Claiborne was indicted for bribery, fraud, and tax evasion. His trial on those charges resulted in a mistrial in April 1984. He was retried in May on just the tax evasion charge, convicted, and sentenced to two years in prison. He was the first federal judge to be convicted of a crime while on the bench. He was also impeached by the U.S. House of Representatives and removed from office. He committed suicide in January 2004.

I don't know if Claiborne ever actually did anything for Tony, but Tony was happy to have him on the bench.

* * *

I'll conclude this chapter with a guy who was a real class act: Moe Dalitz, who got his start as a gangster as a bootlegger during prohibition. In 1949, Dalitz and three of his pals from Cleveland bought the still-under-construction Desert Inn in Vegas. They took the project over from Wilbur Clark, who had started it and then ran into financial problems. Clark was kept on as a figurehead, and the DI opened in 1950 as Wilbur Clark's Desert Inn.

Dalitz was a friend of Jimmy Hoffa's and was responsible for bringing a lot of Teamster money into Vegas starting in 1959. He didn't use all the money to build or expand casinos, though. He also built Sunrise Hospital, shopping malls, and golf courses.

By the time I got to Vegas, Dalitz was more or less retired but was still highly respected and was serving on the board of directors at the Sahara Country Club. Tony had wanted to join the club several years earlier, and Dalitz had sponsored him. Tony spent quite a bit of time there playing gin with the older members. I went with him as a guest several times, and that's when I met Dalitz. He was a real gentleman, very sincere and pleasant to be around.

Tony's country club days ended one day when he and I went to the club and Dalitz said he needed to talk with Tony outside. We went out, and Dalitz said to Tony, "I'm awful sorry about this Tony, but the members have voted you out."

I could tell by Tony's expression he hadn't expected that news. "Voted me out? What are you talking about?" he said.

"You've been in the news a lot lately, and they're afraid of you. They're afraid to refuse to play cards with you, and when they do they're afraid to win. Some of them told me they throw games because they think if they take your money something bad might happen to them. Like I said, I'm very sorry about this."

I have no doubt that he did regret it, but he did what he had to do. Tony knew that and held his cool. "Don't worry about it," he said, "I'll leave."

Dalitz handled an uncomfortable situation as good as he could. Like I said, he was a classy guy.

15

THE STARDUST

I want to share a couple of stories that involve the Stardust. One is about problem resolution, and the other concerns an employee who got whacked, but not by Tony. While I was putting the Hole in the Wall Gang together, Tony told me to make sure I stopped at the Stardust and introduce myself to the casino manager, Lou Salerno. He said Lou would be my contact for anything I needed, and Lou would contact me if there were problems in the casino, like cheating schemes.

I did a lot of stuff with Lou, like arranging for Outfit associates to get comped rooms, meals, drinks, and entertainment when they were in town or even get them a job if they needed one. But one night when I was in the casino Lou approached me with a kind of ticklish matter.

"We've got a problem," he said.

"What kind of problem?"

"Joey DiFronzo, a friend of his, and a pit boss are running a cheat at the blackjack tables. Tell the Little Guy [Tony] what I told you."

I met with Tony and explained the situation.

He said, "Talk with the pit boss first and be nice. Tell him if he gives up the names of everybody involved he'll lose his job at the Stardust, but we'll get him in someplace else. If he doesn't cooperate we'll have to do something different."

I met with the pit boss. (I won't mention his name, but I knew him.) He confirmed the only people involved were Joey and Joey's buddy.

I said, "Good. Don't say a word to anybody about this. Wait a week and then put an application in at the Thunderbird and you'll be hired."

I reported to Tony that Joey DiFronzo and his pal were the only other ones involved.

Tony said, "This could open up a can of worms. Tell Joey we know what he's been doing and that if he gets out of town and stays out, we won't say anything about this to Chicago." I talked with Joey, and he immediately left Vegas and went back to Chicago. His co-cheat got a warning and was banned from all Outfit-controlled properties, and as promised, the pit boss went to work at the Thunderbird.

* * *

Around 1976 or '77, I was in Scottsdale, Arizona, and Paulie Schiro introduced me to a guy named Emil Vaci. I can't recall for sure what Vaci did for a living, but I think he had something to do with a hotel. He and Paulie were involved in some kind of illegal activity at the time. Paulie didn't say what it was, and I didn't want to know.

After I moved to Vegas in 1979 I walked into the Stardust one day and there was Emil Vaci. He walked up to me, shook my hand, and said, "Frankie, how are you?"

"Good, Emil. What are you doing here?"

"I'm working here. I'm a host for the restaurants."

"How'd you land a job like that?"

"The Little Guy got me in."

I saw Paulie not long after that and told him I'd seen Emil. It turned out he and Emil had a falling out and he was really pissed off at him. I didn't think any more about it until 1986, when I heard Emil had been murdered in Arizona. I'd already rolled and become a government witness so I was out of the loop as far as what was going on, but my immediate thought was that it was an Outfit hit and that probably Paulie and Joey Hansen were involved. They had both worked for Tony and did a lot of the heavy work together.

It wasn't until the Family Secrets trial was in progress in July 2007 that the details of Emil's killing came out. News accounts described Emil as a host at a Phoenix restaurant who had the misfortune of getting a grand jury subpoena, and when you had information that could be detrimental to the Outfit, that wasn't a good thing.

Inside the courtroom, Mob hit man Nick Calabrese explained to the jury that he and several other Mob killers stalked Emil for weeks in Phoenix before grabbing him as he left his job one night in June 1986.

Calabrese said he was in a van parked right next to Emil's car waiting for his victim to leave work. When he heard footsteps as Emil approached the van he opened the door and tried to pull Emil inside. Emil fought against the abduction, forcing Calabrese's driver, Joey Hansen, to help get Emil inside.

Calabrese told jurors that as Hansen drove off he pulled out a .22-caliber pistol with a silencer. He said that when Emil realized what was going on he begged for his life. After a misfire, he got the gun working and shot Emil in the head. He then shot Emil a second time just to make sure he was dead.

Whatever information Emil had, the grand jury would never hear it.

16

CARD CREW, SHAKEDOWNS
& AN AVERAGE DAY

Although Tony was in Nevada's Black Book and banned from all casino properties, he still liked to bet and be part of the action. So he bankrolled a crew of card players who played on his behalf in non-Outfit casino poker rooms at places such as the Dunes, Sahara, and Frontier. They would also make sports bets for him in the casino sports books.

His regular gambling crew consisted of a big guy who always wore a cowboy hat and was, of course, called Cowboy. His character was played by actor Craig Vincent in the movie *Casino*. There was also Tony's brother Vince and a guy named Sammy who was a close friend of Tony's.

I was never directly involved in the poker games and don't know exactly how they worked it, but it's my understanding they would enter the card rooms separately and appear not to know each other. They'd make sure to get seated at the same table and play as a team against an unsuspecting player, using various signals to gain an advantage.

Although Tony wasn't happy about being in the Black Book and having to rely on proxy players and betters, one day he told me, "Frankie, when those bastards put me in the Book they actually did me a favor. They've saved me a lot of money by keeping me out of the casinos."

* * *

Tony also had several bookies on the streets taking horse racing and other sporting events action for him. They included Sammy, Herbie Blitzstein, and a guy named Frank Mastriano.

Those guys were good workers and did well for Tony.

But there was a funny incident involving Mastriano that pissed Tony off. Mastriano's son went into one of the parks with his bow and arrow and shot a duck. He didn't kill it, and the duck was running around with the arrow sticking out of him quacking in pain. That drew a lot of attention and was the headline in the newspaper the next day. Tony wasn't happy about it and told Mastriano that he'd better keep his son disarmed. That was the last attempted murder the kid was involved in.

Tony later added a guy named Sarge Ferris, an independent bookie whom we brought into line. Plus, he even had a couple of guys taking book for him in Los Angeles. One was Chris Pettis, and the other was a guy named Mike. They'd come to Vegas at least once a week to give Tony his profits or pick up money to pay off losses.

This was before everyone had a cell phone. Tony knew his landlines were probably tapped, so he used different payphones to keep in touch with his people and keep track of what was going on. Most of the phones were in Vegas, but sometimes they were outside of town.

If other bookies wanted to operate in Vegas they had to pay Tony a tribute known as a "street tax." When Tony found out someone was doing business without kicking anything up to him he'd contact me to straighten things out.

The goal was to make money, not put the rogue bookie out of business. Tony came up with an effective way to do it. Here's an example of how we handled a connected guy from out of town.

Tony told me about a bookie named Dominic who wasn't kicking in. He was from Boston and lived in one of the country clubs. I sent Larry "Lurch" Neumann, Leo Guardino, and Ernie Davino to pay him a visit. They gave me this account of what happened.

When they got to Dominic's house a woman was there with him. They told him to get her out of the room unless he wanted her to know his personal business. After she left,

Lurch grabbed him by the collar and pulled him close.

He said, "Listen, you little greaseball. I know what you're doing out here. I know you're bookmaking. I know you're gambling in these fucking casinos, and you're cheating. You're not cheating in our joints, but we want a piece of your action. Do you understand?"

Obviously scared, Dominic started rattling off the names of people he knew in Boston.

Lurch cut him short. "I don't give a fuck who you're with. You're gonna do what we tell you or you're dead, got it? We'll be back tomorrow for our first payment of $15,000. Do you understand what I'm telling you?"

Dominic did a little moaning, but he agreed to pay.

I called Tony and told him what happened. He loved that kind of stuff.

He said, "I already got a call from this guy's boss in Boston. He said some people were trying to shake his guy down. He asked me to do him a favor and look out for his man. I told him no problem. He's going to start sending Dominic money for me every month to show his appreciation."

This method always worked with bookies who were affiliated with people out of state. However, sometimes they were independents with nobody backing them. Even so, they still had to pay Tony something, or else.

Another time Tony called me and said, "There's a bookmaker named Sarge I want you to grab. This cocksucker's a renegade, and we've got to bring him into line. Tell the bastard that if he wants to continue bookmaking, he'd better start kicking in some money. If he gives you any static, tell him he'd better pay by tomorrow. Send somebody who will scare him. Send Lurch."

I sent Lurch, Leo, and Ernie to deal with Sarge. They read him the riot act. They told me that by the time they finished with him he was so scared they thought he was going to piss his pants.

The next day when I saw Tony he said, "Your guys put

the fear of God into Sarge, and he came to me asking for protection. Now I own him. I can gamble into that bastard for free now, got it?"

On the rare occasions when a bookie couldn't or wouldn't pay the street tax, we'd run him out of town.

* * *

Another guy we shook down was a former Chicagoan named Jack Rizzo. He was a big drug dealer in Vegas, always wore a lot of jewelry, and even carried a gold cigarette lighter. I met him a few times, and one day I mentioned him to Tony and that Rizzo was dealing a lot of coke.

Tony said, "He is, huh? Well, he's not giving us a piece of his action, and that's gotta stop. You and your guys pay him a visit and tell him Chicago wants 500 grand, if he wants to stay in business."

I laughed. "Tony, I doubt if this guy's got that kind of money. Maybe a couple hundred, but I think that's about it."

"He probably doesn't. We want to throw a scare into him, and then we can come back with a lower price. Tell him what I told you, and we'll see what he says."

I sent Leo and Ernie Davino to talk with Jack. They reported back to me that he said he didn't have a half million. He pleaded for a few days to see how much he could raise. Leo told him, "We're just doing what Chicago told us. We'll tell them you're going to come up with some money in a few days. Is that right?"

Scared, Rizzo said, "Yeah, yeah, tell them I need a couple of days."

I went with Leo and Ernie when they talked with Rizzo again. He said, "Frank, why are you doing this to me?"

"It's not me, Jack, it's Chicago. They heard you're selling a lot of high-quality drugs out here, and they want their cut."

"I haven't got a half million," he whined.

"I understand. Give me $300,000, and I'll tell them that's

all you can afford."

"That's still too much."

"I'll tell you what, Jack. I'll stall Chicago for a week. You get together all the money you can, and I'll tell them that's all you can afford."

"Thanks, Frank, I appreciate that. I'll do the best I can."

"Okay, but remember one thing. Don't have me go to bat for you and then find out you held back. Chicago wouldn't like that and neither would I."

A week later Rizzo called and told me the most he could pay was $50,000. I said, "If that's all you can do, it's all you can do. I'll send Ernie and Leo to your place tomorrow to pick up the money."

Tony wasn't happy. "Fifty fucking grand? That's all that bastard is going to pay?"

I said, "He says that's all he's got."

"I'll tell you what, Frankie, have your guys tie the prick up. Tell him Chicago wants 300. Take the fifty and all his fucking jewelry. Tell him when he comes up with the rest of the money he'll get his jewelry back."

Leo and Ernie followed orders. They untied Rizzo after they had the cash and all the jewelry from his safe, which we estimated as being worth about $100,000. "Call us when you have the rest of the cash, and we'll give you your stuff back," Leo said.

A few days later Rizzo called. He said that he'd only been able to raise an additional twenty grand. He wanted to know if Chicago would accept that and if we'd give him his jewelry back. After checking with Tony, I told him it was a deal. Because of what happened to him the last time Leo and Ernie were at his house, Rizzo insisted on meeting in a public place—the coffee shop at the Stardust.

In the coffee shop Rizzo sat at the counter between Ernie and me, with Leo at the end. What Rizzo didn't know was that we had another guy at a table watching us. When Rizzo passed Ernie the envelope containing the money, our friend walked past, took the money, and kept walking out the door.

Rizzo said, "Where's my jewelry?"

Ernie said, "There ain't any fucking jewelry."

Rizzo started to protest, and when he pointed his finger at Ernie, Ernie grabbed it and snapped it. He told Rizzo, "You're beat. Give it up."

As we got up to leave I said to Rizzo, "It might be a good idea if you moved out of Nevada." He disappeared a few days later, and I never saw or heard of him again. We kept the nicest pieces of jewelry for ourselves and sold the rest for about $25,000. Tony took 20 percent of the total take, and Leo, Ernie, and I cut up the rest. Nothing went to Chicago.

* * *

Not all our muscle jobs were done to directly benefit Tony. On occasion he would ask us to do a favor for a friend.

Jasper Speciale ran the Leaning Tower of Pizza in Vegas. He was affiliated with New York, and in addition to the restaurant, he was a bookie and loan shark. Jasper was highly respected, and Tony liked him a lot.

Tony came to me and said a guy owed Jasper $800 or $900 in lost bets and wasn't paying. He said, "Frankie, I want you to make sure this prick pays Jasper what he owes. The guy goes to Chicago Joe's restaurant on Main Street every Friday and Saturday. Talk to him."

Tony gave me the deadbeat's name, physical description, and what kind of car he drove. That Friday, Larry Neumann, Leo Guardino, and I went to the restaurant and hung around until the guy showed up. I asked him to talk with us outside, and in a nice way, I said we'd appreciate it if he paid Jasper what he owed him.

The guy didn't know us or that Larry had a very violent temper. When he got a little arrogant, Larry grabbed him by the lapels on his jacket and shoved him up against the wall. With his face inches away, he said, "Listen, you fucking prick, I want that money you owe Jasper paid by tomorrow or you'll never enjoy another day on this earth."

Jasper got his money the next day.

* * *

It seems that whenever I do a public or private talk someone will ask: What was it like to be a mobster? What was your lifestyle? Since we're talking about Tony, I'll tell you what his average day was like.

Mobsters work a seven-day week, and weekends are the same as any other day—even for a boss like Tony. His average day in Vegas was pretty much like this. He was a night guy and would be out until around 5:30 in the morning, taking care of business, meeting people, socializing, or seeing his girlfriends. When he got home his number one priority was to get Vincent up, fix him breakfast, and get him off to school. He truly loved the kid, and in that respect he was a perfect father. After that he'd nap for a few hours.

Starting around noon Tony's gambling crew—usually three or four guys—would start showing up one at a time to turn over their winnings or, if they had lost, get funding for their next venture, have a cup of coffee, and then leave. Afterward, Tony would play gin rummy with whoever was still around or stopped in. The card game would end around three or so, and Tony would pick Vincent up from school and bring him home. Sometimes, if there was no afternoon card game, he'd leave his house earlier to make phone calls or stop at the Gold Rush or my restaurant to bullshit and give me any necessary instructions.

By around six o'clock he'd be back home for dinner. If for some reason he was late, Nancy would call around and try to track him down. So all of Tony's friends would lie to her and claim not to know where Tony was. When she got tired of that runaround she'd get in her car and start looking for him.

Because Tony didn't like to drive he'd generally meet with somebody who would chauffeur him around. That meant that even though Nancy found Tony's car parked near a particular location, it didn't necessarily mean he was actually there. She did catch up with him on occasion, though, and then the fur would fly.

Later in the evening we'd meet at the My Place bar to do a little light drinking, and sometimes one of Tony's girlfriends would meet him there. They'd hang around a while and then take off. He also met with people there to discuss business, so we had a guy come in every so often and check for bugs. Alan Dorfman used to meet with Tony there. He'd stop in my restaurant and ask me to let Tony know he was in town. I'd go to a pay phone, call Tony, and tell him he had a visitor.

The Hole in the Wall Gang crew wasn't allowed to hang with Tony. If they were in the same place they could say hello, but that was it. Tony wanted to keep a distance between him and them for everybody's good. All instructions for them from Tony went through me.

It was a good life for all of us.

17

SHERWIN 'JERRY' LISNER

A guy I met early on in Vegas was named Jerry Lisner. He ended up playing a major role in the future lives of Tony and me.

One of the spots a lot of the guys hung out at was Jubilation, a lounge on East Harmon. I was in there one night when someone introduced me to Lisner. I'd seen him around and knew a little about him. He was a wannabe gangster—a con artist, scammer, and hustler—and the kind of guy I had no fucking use for. Lisner knew some things about me, too—mainly that I was connected with Tony Spilotro—and he wanted to meet me. I wasn't real excited about it, but sometimes things just happen.

After we talked for a while Lisner started getting around to his point. He said he was setting up a scam to run on a guy in Florida and needed my help.

"Why me?" I asked him.

"This guy is slightly connected, and I know you're with Tony Spilotro. Having you involved will give me credibility and make it more likely he'll go for the deal."

"What makes you think I'm tied in with Tony?"

"That's what I hear."

I didn't admit or deny what he said about Tony and me. Instead, I asked for the details of the scam he wanted me to help him with.

"This guy's got a lot of money," Lisner said. "I'm sure we can take him in a money- laundering deal."

"What kind of money are we talking?"

"I think we can get $175,000 out of him."

"How are you gonna do it?"

"Here's the setup. I'll tell him I've got some money— about $400,000—that I want to wash because the serial numbers are in sequence. I'll say I'm willing to swap my cash for $175,000 in clean money. Once the guy bites, we'll pull the scam. I know how to do it, and I've got a brother-in-law that's a cop in Washington, D.C., who'll work with us." Although I didn't like Lisner, I liked the sound of the money. I said, "How do I fit in?"

"You'd help me set it up and then come with me to D.C. to exchange the money. We'll fix up an attaché case with a row of hundred-dollar bills on top of stacks of singles. You give the guy a quick peek in the case, and it will look like it holds a lot more money than it does. You'll swap cases, and we'll leave with the 175 grand. As the other guy is walking away with the case he got from us, my brother-in-law will arrest him. He'll confiscate the money and then turn him loose. The victim will be thankful he didn't go to jail. We'll end up with both cases, and the sucker will never even realize what happened. We'll be home free."

I liked the idea of using a case of flash money. Not having a lot of our own money at risk if something went wrong and the bait case got confiscated by the law was appealing. And if the victim insisted on actually counting the money before switching cases, we could just rob him and he wouldn't be able to do much about it. If he went to the cops, how would he explain having that amount of money and what he was trying to do with it when he got robbed?

Even though I liked the plan I wanted to run it past Tony before I committed to getting involved. I told Lisner I'd think it over and get back to him.

I got in touch with Tony and told him Lisner's pitch. He said, "Sounds a little corny, doesn't it? On the other hand, some people are so greedy they'd go for a deal like that. But us? As much as I love money, we're a little sharper than them guys. We wouldn't go for a deal like that. We'd know right away this guy was trying to fuck us.

"Here's what I want you to do. Go back and tell Lisner you thought it over, and it sounds like a good idea. Whatever you do, don't tell him you talked with me about it. Tell him you want $75,000 because you have to take care of your people. He can have the $100,000 and take care of his people. If he doesn't want to go for that, tell him to go fuck himself."

Lisner agreed to my terms, and we got the ball rolling. We flew to D.C. and were spending $300 a night for hotel rooms waiting for the Florida guy to meet us for the money swap. But he wasn't as stupid as Lisner thought—he was suspicious and kept stalling us. We ended up reducing the amount of money he'd have to put up and he still wouldn't go for it. The whole deal fell through.

I was pissed off about everything and was especially mad at Lisner. He sensed it, and on the flight back to Vegas he apologized. "I'm real sorry about this thing blowing up on us. I thought for sure we had him."

I said, "Time is money, and we blew a lot of both. But shit happens, so forget about it."

"I'll tell you what. I've got a Quaalude deal in the works. I can cut you in on that, and you'll at least get your money back."

"I don't handle drugs," I said.

"There are a lot of outs for them, and you won't have to touch them, yourself. I'll get you 5,000 Quaaludes for five grand. You'll be able to sell them for ten, doubling your money."

It sounded too good to pass up, and I agreed. The next day I had the Quaaludes and told Tony about them. He said, "Get rid of them fucking things quick. I don't want any drugs around."

I sold the Quaaludes to a local kid for $10,000. My half covered what I'd spent on the botched money-laundering scam and gave me a nice profit, besides. I didn't like Lisner so I decided to stiff him for the $5,000 he wanted for the Quaaludes and gave it to Tony instead. I told Lisner I had to dump the drugs before I could sell them because the cops were on me. Lisner probably didn't believe it, but I didn't care whether he did or not.

I figured I'd heard the last of Jerry Lisner. I hadn't, though, and he turned up again like a bad penny. The trouble started when Lisner was arrested by the FBI on July 11, 1979, and charged with interstate transportation of stolen property, aiding and abetting, grand larceny, and conspiracy. He was free on $75,000 bail and was scheduled to go on trial October 29 in U.S. District Court in Washington, D.C.

In the late summer I was at my restaurant when I got a call from a Joe Pignatello, owner of the Villa d'Este. "Joe Pig," as he was known, was a Chicago guy and a friend of Sam Giancana's. The word was that Sam set Joe Pig up with the restaurant. Because it was known as a connected place, all kinds of people stopped there when they were in Vegas, including lawyers.

Joe said he needed to talk with me about something important, and I told him to come over. He said a lawyer from Washington, D.C., had been in his place and told him that Jerry Lisner was playing ball with the feds to get a plea deal. He'd been in front of a grand jury there and mentioned my and Tony's names.

I thanked Joe and then got hold of Tony. "I don't like it, Frankie," he said. "If this shit is true, it looks like they're trying to indict one or both of us."

"What do you want to do?"

"For right now, nothing. I want to check into this thing myself, and I'll get back to you."

A few days later I heard from Tony. He'd confirmed what Joe Pig had told me and a little more. "Listen to me, Frankie. This fuckin' Lisner is cooperating with the grand jury in Washington. He's giving testimony about you and your affiliation with me. And he's talking about that deal in Washington [the money laundering scam] you tried to pull. Subpoenas are gonna be issued."

Tony's information was solid. The very next day the FBI served me with a subpoena to appear before the grand jury in Washington. After they left I called Tony. "What should I do, Tony? Should I make up a bullshit story? Should I take the Fifth [exercise my right against self-incrimination] and force them to offer me immunity?"

"Get a lawyer out of D.C. and make up a story. We'll deal with Lisner later."

I went to Washington and retained a lawyer. After discussing my testimony with him I was interviewed by a U.S. attorney and some FBI agents. They gave me a grilling, but I stuck to my made-up story. I testified the same way when I went before the grand jury.

When I got back to Vegas I told my associate Larry Neumann (a six-time killer) what was going on with Lisner. "Let's kill the fucker right now," he said.

"We can't just go around whacking people without permission. I've got to find out what Tony wants to do first. And if he wants Lisner hit, he'll have to clear it with Chicago. While we're waiting, try to get close to Lisner's wife, Jeanne, at the Aladdin [where she was a cocktail waitress]. See what you can learn from her. If we want to feed any bullshit to Jerry, we'll do it through her."

Larry did what I said and became buddies with the Lisners, but he didn't like them. He told me that when it was time to hit Lisner, he wanted to do the job. "I want to kill both of them, though. He's got it coming, and she's a no good fucking bitch. She's got to go, too."

Tony finally made up his mind about Lisner, and when he did, he was emphatic. He told me, "I want him fuckin' whacked. And if *you* don't do it, *I* will."

"Take it easy, Tony. I'll handle it."

"I just want to make sure you understand that I want that cocksucker taken care of. I got the okay from Chicago, and it's gotta be done."

"It'll be done. Should I take Larry with me?"

"No, leave Larry out of it. Have Wayne [Matecki] come in from Chicago."

"Okay. I'll contact Wayne. Anything else?"

"Yeah, get hold of Lisner. Meet him for a few drinks or something so he gets comfortable with you being around him."

I contacted Lisner and invited him and his wife to meet me at the My Place Lounge next to my restaurant. We had a good time, laughing, and joking. Tony stopped by and turned on the charm, making the Lisners feel even more at ease. It was time to move to the next stage.

I drove to Los Angeles and flew from the Burbank airport to Chicago. I made contact with Wayne and briefed him on the plan to murder Lisner. He packed his bag, and we caught a plane back to Burbank and then drove to Vegas, where I already had a work car stashed in the underground parking garage of my condo. We assembled the rest of the necessary equipment: a .22 pistol, a police radio, and walkie-talkies. Everything was ready.

On October 10, 1979, I called Lisner. "Jerry, I need to discuss something with you, but I don't want to do it on the phone. Can we get together tonight?"

"Sure. Why don't you stop by my house, and we'll talk."

"Good. This is private, though, so—"

Lisner cut me off. "Jeannie has to work. I'll be alone, so you don't have to worry."

"Thanks, Jerry. I'll be over."

After dark Wayne and I put our radios and walkie-talkies in the work car and headed for the Lisner house at 2303 Rawhide Avenue. I concealed the gun in my waistband. When we got to Lisner's, I told Wayne to wait in the car and I went to the door and rang the bell. Lisner responded right away and let me in. We stood in the hallway for a few seconds making small talk, and then I used a ruse to get Lisner away from the door. "What was that?"

"What was what?" Lisner said.

"I heard a noise. I thought you were alone."

"Nobody's here but me. Come on, let's take a look."

I followed Lisner into the living room. I couldn't wear

gloves without looking suspicious to Lisner, so I was very careful not to touch anything that could retain my fingerprints.

"See, nobody's here but you and me," Lisner said.

"Maybe the noise came from outside."

Lisner then led the way toward the rear of the house to check the backyard. As we passed through the dining room I pulled my gun. I fired two rounds into the back of Lisner's head from point-blank range. Instead of going down, he turned around and said, "What the ... why?" Then he started to run through the house toward the garage.

I caught up with him and emptied the rest of the bullets into his head. He fell but was still alive, still moving. I had trouble believing what was happening. I got on top of Lisner and held him down while looking around the room for something to use as a weapon. I saw a knife on a counter next to the door leading to the garage and made a grab for it; it was just out of reach. Next I spotted an electric water cooler that was within my grasp. I ripped the cord out of the cooler to strangle Lisner with, but when I wrapped it around his neck the cord broke. *Unbelievable!*

I got up and dragged Lisner into the den. He was still conscious and aware of what was going on. "My wife knows you're here! She's going to know you did this!" he said.

At that time Wayne came into the house; he was carrying an extra magazine of ammo with him. I reloaded the gun, put pillows from a couch over Lisner's head to muffle the gunshots, and emptied it into his head again. It had taken ten fucking rounds, but Lisner was finally dead. We dragged him outside to the pool and dumped him in. The body floated for a few seconds, then sank to the bottom.

We went back into the house; there was blood everywhere. We wiped everything off and then checked the house for any security cameras or recorders. There weren't any. We also looked for any papers or address books that might have been incriminating and didn't find any of those either.

After completing the search we drove back to my condo.

We showered, scrubbed our hands with kitchen cleanser, and cut the clothes we'd been wearing into little pieces. Then we drove the work car into the desert, scattering the dismantled gun and scraps of clothing. Finally, we parked the work car in my parking garage and used my personal vehicle to drive Wayne to McCarran Airport. He was on a plane back to Chicago that same night.

The hit was big news all over town. The next night I met Tony at the My Place; we talked in the parking lot. "I've got a couple of questions about Lisner," Tony said. "We'll talk about him now but never again after tonight. Understand?"

"Sure. Go ahead."

"How come you guys dumped him in the pool?"

"We wanted to get rid of some of the blood and any prints we might have left on his clothes."

"That was a bit theatrical, wasn't it?"

"We did what we figured we had to do."

"How come you had to fire so many shots?"

"I was hitting him right in the fuckin' head every time. But that small caliber didn't work well, didn't do the job."

"Maybe you should have used half-loads," Tony joked.

"Half-loads? This fucking guy wouldn't die with full loads. What good would half-loading have done?"

We never talked about Lisner again.

* * *

In addition to Lisner, something else happened in 1979 that would later play a role in my relationship with Tony. I fell in love.

Nick Costanza was a tipster who turned us on to good scores in return for a percentage of the take. I hired his daughter Elaine and son Jerry to work in my Upper Crust restaurant. Elaine was very sharp and extremely loyal—very important qualities to a guy like me. We got along well, and it wasn't long before I was sleeping with her. On January 1, 1980, we were married. Our reception was held in the Moby Dick restaurant in the Stardust, and the casino comped it all. It was kind of funny because the Metro detectives who were doing surveillance on us sat a few tables away from the wedding party drinking soda, while we were eating steak and drinking champagne.

When things started going sour between Tony and me, it was Elaine who saw the signs first. I laughed off her warnings and told her she was crazy. She wasn't.

18

PUTTING ON THE HEAT

I mentioned that Las Vegas Metro usually had Tony, me, and my crew under surveillance. They weren't the only agency interested in us, though; we were at the top of the FBI's list as well. Prior to me moving to Vegas the FBI didn't trust Metro, and they worked independently. However, when John McCarthy took over as sheriff in January 1979 they made peace and were soon fully cooperating with each other. They made a formidable team and put a lot of heat on us.

I'll talk about one of their joint operations shortly, but first I want to tell you about an FBI wiretap that resulted in some verbal fireworks and nearly a fistfight between Tony and an FBI agent.

The feds were really hung up on what we talked about inside the Upper Crust. They figured we planned scores and talked about all our crimes there and decided they needed to get a bug inside to get us admitting everything on tape.

They were wrong. We knew the restaurant would be a prime target for them so we made it a point to never discuss business there. If they'd have asked me I'd have told them bugging the place would be a waste of time. But they didn't ask me and placed a camera and mic in the back room. The bad news for them was that we found their equipment less than a day after they installed it.

It was a Sunday afternoon, and I was supposed to meet Leo Guardino at the restaurant to go on a burglary. He got there early and decided to go in the back room and take a snooze before I picked him up. He climbed on top of a chest-type freezer, and before he closed his eyes he saw something shiny in the ceiling vent right above his head. He pushed up a ceiling tile and found the bug. Then he called me. Without going into detail, he told me I needed to get to the restaurant right away.

After Leo showed me the bug we went outside to talk. I told him to go into the crawl space above the ceiling and follow the wires to the monitoring equipment. He was back in a few minutes and said he followed the wires to a real estate office a couple of stores away. We both went into the crawl space to the real estate office where I ripped the wires out of the equipment. When we crawled back to the restaurant I removed the camera and microphone.

I didn't think there were any more bugs, but just in case I went to My Place and called Tony. He said, "Bring that camera to my house, and we'll check it and find out who it belongs to."

When I got to Tony's, Joe Blasko—a former Metro cop who was fired after an FBI wiretap caught him giving police information to Tony—was there. Blasko checked the camera and found a metal tag that had been painted over. He removed the paint with alcohol and it said "Property of the U.S. Government."

Tony went berserk. *"The fuckin' FBI!"* he said.

I asked, "What are we gonna do now?"

Tony pointed at the camera. "I know a Jew who can use shit like that. I'll give it to him. Then we'll sit back and see how the G is going to handle this."

Elaine and me had just got to the Upper Crust on Monday morning when I looked out the window and saw a sea of suits outside. No doubt they were the FBI agents looking for their equipment. I'd already told Elaine about the bugs, and now I told her to be careful what she said if any of the suits came inside.

I took a seat at one of the tables. I had the microphone in my pocket, so I removed it and set it in an ashtray in case they searched me. Elaine noticed the move, came over, and took the ashtray. She removed the mic, went next door to My Place, and flushed it down the toilet. The suits didn't pay any attention to her when she walked past them.

A couple of minutes later five or six of the agents came

inside. Two of them went to the pay phone, and the others sat at separate tables. None of them said anything, so I walked over to one of them and asked, "Are you with the FBI?" The guy laughed. "Me? With the FBI? No way." "I know you guys have to identify yourselves if you're asked." "I don't know what you're talking about." I knew it was a lie but decided not to challenge him any further and returned to my seat. One of the suits walked by me and smirked but didn't say anything. The agents hung around a few more minutes and then left.

The smirker came back in about an hour. He identified himself as Charlie Parsons and said he was one of the bosses in the FBI's Las Vegas office. He had another agent with him who he introduced as Emmett Michaels. Parsons asked me to step outside to talk. He said, "We want our camera back."

"I don't have your fuckin' camera."

"We know damn well you've got it. If you don't give it back, we'll ride you day and night."

"You can go fuck yourself. I wouldn't give you the camera back now, even if I did have it."

"Contact your lawyer and have him give me a call," Parsons said. He and Michaels left, but they weren't happy.

I called Tony and told him what happened. Tony said he was going to call Oscar Goodman for advice and would get back to me. It turned out Goodman was out of town, so Tony called Dominic Gentile—a lawyer originally from Chicago—to represent him in Goodman's absence. Gentile called Parsons and arranged for a meeting at the Upper Crust that night. Me, Tony, Gentile, Parsons, and Michaels all got together to talk.

Parsons said the camera was government property and had been placed legally with a court order. While he was talking, Tony was standing with his hand stuck inside his shirt. Michaels said to him, "You look like a little Caesar standing there like that."

Tony didn't like lawmen. He said, "Fuck you, you bald-headed motherfucker."

Michaels and Tony glared at each other, and the tension built. Knowing Tony the way I did, I figured this was a situation that could easily escalate into a fistfight. I said to the agents, "Look, this is my place, and your beef is with me. If you've got anything to say, say it to me, not Tony." That seemed to defuse the situation, and there was no more conversation between Michaels and Tony.

After some negotiating, the agents said that if they got their camera back, that would be the end of it. Gentile called me and Tony aside to talk it over. I wanted to play hardball, but Tony figured if the camera was returned, the feds would back off a little. I told Parsons he'd get his camera back, but that the microphone was somewhere in Lake Mead.

That night I picked up the camera from Tony's Jewish friend and got it to Parsons. Unlike Tony, I wasn't expecting Parsons to back off and knew I hadn't seen the last of him and his men.

* * *

While all this was going on, there was a big blowup between Lefty and Geri over her affair with Tony. The incident was included in *Casino*, but they left out an important fact: Nancy Spilotro was in the middle of it. Denny Griffin reported it this way in *The Battle for Las Vegas*:

"It was September 8, 1980. Geri Rosenthal had been out all night and when she got home at around 9 a.m., she was high on drugs, booze, or both. Finding herself locked out of the house, she became enraged. Getting back into her Mercedes, she repeatedly rammed her car into the rear of Lefty's parked Cadillac. There was damage to each vehicle, but they both remained drivable. The commotion brought Lefty out to his front porch and a number of neighbors onto their lawns. A security guard called the police.

"At the sight of her husband Geri exited her car and took up a position on the lawn, shouting at him. She said the FBI wanted to talk with her and she just might go see them. She also announced that Tony Spilotro was her 'sponsor' (protector) and wanted to know what Lefty planned to do about it.

"During her tirade a police car pulled up and the officers tried using their verbal skills to calm down the out-of-control woman. Soon after the police got there, another car arrived. Nancy Spilotro was the driver.

"She remembered that morning very well. 'Lefty called me and said that Geri was outside the house raising hell. He asked if I'd come over and see if I could help. I went right over. I was still in my pajamas, covered by a robe.'

"While the police continued trying to reason with Geri, she pulled a pearl-handled revolver from under her clothing and waved it in the general direction of her husband. The police officers dove for cover behind their car. Neighbors scurried for safety. Lefty remained where he was, seemingly unable to move. That was when the five-foot, 97-pound Nancy Spilotro sprang into action. She launched herself at the other woman.

"Nancy recalled with a laugh, 'I must have been quite a sight, flying through the air in my pajamas and robe.' Funny or not, the diminutive Spilotro was effective. She wrestled the larger woman to the ground and disarmed her. With the danger over and additional police cars on the scene, the spectators returned to their positions to watch the rest of the action."

As I said earlier, Nancy Spilotro was a spitfire.

19

BERTHA'S

There were several events that contributed to the demise of the Outfit in Las Vegas, to the end of my friendship with Tony, and, I believe, to his death. In my opinion, the most important occurrence was our attempt to rob a store named Bertha's.

Not long after I got into Vegas, Joey DiFronzo took me to a high-end store called Bertha's Gifts and Home Furnishings on East Sahara. He explained that anybody who was anybody in Vegas bought their stuff at Bertha's and their vault was always filled with quality jewelry and cash. It would be a difficult place to burglarize but would make a hell of a score.

I went inside the store to check it out while Joey waited in the car. They had a good alarm system with motion detectors but no cameras. I saw where the vault was located and stepped off the distances to various walls to get a decent estimate of its location.

When I got back to the car we talked about the best way to rob the store. Joey thought breaking through a wall would be the way to go. I disagreed. The only wall you could access was on the side of the building facing Sahara. You'd need a work truck to carry all the tools you'd have to use and would have to park it next to the wall to conceal the break-in. A truck parked there would be so out of place it would get spotted by a police patrol or reported by a citizen very quickly. We talked a little more and then kind of passed on it.

However, as time went by the cops were on us all the time, making it a lot harder to steal. They were always parked outside my restaurant and that cut into my business. On top of that, I was getting arrested more often and had to keep coming up with money for bonds. By the spring of 1981 my financial situation had deteriorated to a dangerous point and I needed to do something quick. Knocking off Bertha's seemed like the best chance for a score big enough to let me get my head back above water financially. I started working on a plan that would do the job with a good chance we could get away clean.

* * *

Money and the law weren't my only problems, though. I wasn't happy about a thief and burglar alarm guy from Chicago who showed up and started hanging around My Place and the Upper Crust—his name was Sal Romano. There was something about him that didn't seem right to me. I didn't trust him, but Sal made friends with Tony. He installed alarms in Tony's house and Tony liked him, so I had to let him come around but didn't get too close. Some of the other guys thought he was okay, though, and Ernie and Leo took him along on some scores. It turned out that Sal would be the guy who helped bring us all down and changed the history of organized crime in Las Vegas.

* * *

When I completed my Bertha's plan I met with Tony. I told him what I wanted to do and how it could be done. I said we could take Bertha's by going through the roof right over the vault. That way we'd avoid any alarms. When we got inside, we'd take only the stuff in the vault and not roam around the store—that would mean we'd be in and out pretty quick. I'd learned that other jewelry stores near Bertha's stashed some of their cash and jewelry in Bertha's vault when they were closed for holidays—making a long holiday weekend the best time to do the burglary. It happened that in 1981, the Fourth of July fell on Saturday and the stores would shut down on Friday.

Tony liked the idea, but he had some questions. "How much do you figure will be in the vault?"

"Between cash and jewelry we're looking at $1 million or more."

"What about fencing the jewelry?"

"We'll have somebody drive the stuff to Chicago right after the job, and your brother Michael can get rid of it for us. If we do it that way, it'll be long gone before anybody knows it's even missing. Can you set that up with Michael?"

"I'll be able to take care of it, don't worry. How many guys are you planning to use?"

"I think we can do it with five. Leo, Ernie, and Wayne Matecki will do the burglary. After they cut the hole in the roof, two of them will drop down onto the vault. If it's encased in steel, they'll have to cut through it with a torch. If it's just cinder block, they can chop their way in. They'll pass the merchandise up to the guy on the roof and go out the same hole after they clean out the vault. While they're doing that, Larry and me will run counter surveillance in separate cars. "

"What about taking Joe [Blasko] along?"

I wasn't a fan of Blasko. He was a former cop and once a cop, always a cop. I said, "What do we need him for?"

"You know the fucking cops and FBI are always on us. You've gotta have Joe with you to monitor police calls and see what they're up to. *I want* Joe in on the job."

I wasn't happy, but Tony was the boss and I had to accept his decision. "Okay, Joe's in."

"It sounds good, Frankie. Let me think it over, and I'll let you know."

"Sure. But if we're gonna do it on July Fourth we don't have much time to get ready. It's not only a long weekend, but the cops will have their hands full dealing with big crowds and fireworks displays. And if we don't do it then, the next chance won't be until Labor Day. I need something sooner than that."

"I'm not gonna keep you hanging, Frankie. While you're waiting, reach out to Wayne and make sure he's available and put together a list of the equipment you'll need."

Other than the Blasko thing, I was pleased with Tony's response. I put together the list of equipment and would be ready to move fast as soon as Tony gave me the word.

* * *

While I waited, Sal Romano seemed to be haunting me. Whether I was in the Upper Crust or My Place it seemed that every time I turned around he was there.

And then two Chicago cops I'd known for years showed up in Las Vegas on vacation. They stopped at the Upper Crust to say "hello" and see if I could get them comped at the Stardust. While we were talking, one of them said, "We hear Sal Romano's living here now. Ever see him around?"

"Yeah, he's around. What about him?"

"We don't know about this guy. We busted him at O'Hare Airport with a load of furs he'd stolen here in Vegas. Because we had him for interstate transportation, we turned him over to the feds. Well, they haven't done anything with it. He hasn't even been indicted. We're looking at this Romano as maybe being an informant now. We're not sure, but it doesn't look right. We figured we'd pass this on to you while we were here."

As far as I was concerned that confirmed my suspicions about Sal. When I told Tony what the cops said, he sort of shrugged it off by saying, "You gotta take this stuff at face value, Frankie. How much can you trust these guys? They're cops!"

Shortly after that Tony gave me the go-ahead on Bertha's. He would get an end of the score but wouldn't actually be at the scene. The Outfit would also get a cut. But even with all the payouts, my piece would be enough to get the monkey off my back.

We only had a few weeks to put everything together, and there was a lot to be done. I knew that as soon as the burglary was reported we'd be at the top of Metro's list of suspects, so we had to make arrangements to get an acetylene torch and radio equipment from out of town so they'd be hard for the cops to connect to us. We also needed a ladder, pry bars, drills, a hacksaw, metal cutters, and duffel bags to carry the merchandise. And I had to find a vehicle to haul the equipment to Bertha's and a van for Blasko to use for his radio stuff.

Things were falling into place nicely, and we were just days away from doing the job when I got about the worst news I could imagine. Ernie Davino told me he'd asked Sal Romano to come along on the Bertha's score. I was so fucking mad I could hardly see straight. I screamed at him, "You had no goddamn business bringing him in! Tony and me make those decisions, not you."

"I only asked him because I figured he could help out with the alarms."

"We don't fucking need him. We've got everything covered. I don't trust the son of a bitch, and I don't want him in on the job."

I went to Tony and gave him the news. He wasn't happy about it, either, but he said, "If Sal is bad like you think, the damage is already done— he knows. You might as well let him come along."

"I'd rather just pass on the whole thing."

"There's too much money involved, and it's too close to call it off now."

"Sal installed a burglar alarm in your house. I wouldn't doubt that he bugged your place."

"If he did, the cops would have arrested me by now. Sal did a nice job putting that system in for me, Frankie; he's a good man. You've just got a hard-on for him for some reason."

"He's bad fucking news, and I don't want any part of him."

"I'll tell you what. Take him on the job but have Larry

watch him. Tell Larry that if Sal does anything funny, he should take him out."

That was that—Sal was in. Now my crew was me and six other guys. I trusted four of them, but I didn't like Blasko or Romano and figured either or both could be snitches.

* * *

On the night of July Fourth we arrived at Bertha's around nine o'clock. Leo, Wayne, and Ernie were driving an old station wagon we got to haul the equipment in and pulled it up on the side of the store. Larry and me were in separate vehicles equipped with CBs and planned to keep cruising the area looking for any police activity or anything suspicious. The whole crew had walkie-talkies. Sal Romano wanted to drive around alone to do counter-surveillance, but I told him he had to ride with Larry.

Joe Blasko was in a van I borrowed from a guy I knew. He parked in a shopping center across from Bertha's with his radio equipment. He had a police scanner to monitor known Metro and FBI frequencies. He also had a CB radio and walkie-talkie. I was satisfied with the setup and figured we had more or less neutralized Sal.

Leo, Wayne, and Ernie unloaded the station wagon and hauled everything up onto the roof. Then they moved the car a short distance away so as not to draw attention.

The first sign of trouble came when they were almost ready to break through the roof and Larry told Sal to move the station wagon closer to the building so it could be loaded quickly. I heard Sal radio back to Larry that the wagon wouldn't start and he couldn't move it. I swung by the station wagon to see what was going on. There was no sign of Sal. I got into the wagon and turned the key—it started right up. I radioed Larry, "There's nothing wrong with this goddamn car. Where's Sal?"

"I don't know; he's not with me."

I knew in my gut we were in big trouble. *"Find the son of a bitch!"*

Right about then Leo radioed that he was inside the store. "I can see the vault. It's only cinder block!"

As Leo was announcing the good news, I checked my rearview mirror and found a van right on my ass. I pulled into the shopping center parking lot where there were a lot of people around and pulled over. A bunch of guys jumped out of the van hollering they were FBI and Metro. They got me out of my car and told me to put my hands on the hood and not move. After they searched me and the car I was handcuffed, put in their van, and read my rights. As we were leaving the parking lot for Bertha's, I heard a radio transmission that Blasko had been captured along with all the radio equipment. When we pulled up in front of the store I saw Leo, Wayne, and Ernie face down on the concrete with their hands cuffed behind their backs. Larry had been picked up, too. Everybody was accounted for—except Sal Romano.

Almost as soon as we were booked into jail, I started looking for Sal. He wasn't in the lockup. Nobody had seen him, and nobody knew where he was. One of the guys said he must have gotten away.

I said, "Bullshit! He's a fucking informant, and he set us up."

Joe Blasko didn't believe it. "Tony would never have let that happen."

I said, "I never trusted that bastard, and I told Tony about it several times. But Tony knew it all, and here we are."

We were put in adjoining cells so we were still able to talk. But we were afraid the cells might be bugged and were real careful about what we said. Blasko whined that he couldn't stay in jail because he had obligations. He asked if he could get bonded out first. I didn't give a fuck who got out first and would be glad to get rid of him. I assumed Tony was already working on getting *all* of us out—but he wasn't.

I used one of my phone calls to talk to my father-in-law,

Nick Costanza, at the Upper Crust. He said Sal had phoned, wanting to know if he was the only one that escaped. When Nick asked how he had managed to get away, Sal hung up on him.

Then I called our regular bondsman to find out why he wasn't at the jail working on getting us out. He said my call was the first he'd heard about the arrests. Tony hadn't contacted him. *What the fuck was going on?* The bondsman finally showed up and got the guys out one at a time—Blasko first. Soon, everyone was out but me. The bondsman said I wasn't getting out because the judge had revoked my bond on another case. I called my lawyer, and he got me a hearing before a more liberal judge. He released me on yet another $100,000 bond. In the end, I put up all the bail money for the whole crew. Tony hadn't contributed anything—another bad sign.

I was beginning to lose confidence in Tony. Getting taken in by the likes of Sal Romano was inexcusable for a guy who had been around as much as Tony. And his failure to lift a finger to get me or any of the guys out of jail was not the way a boss was supposed to treat his crew. Still, Tony was my friend and I was gonna stick with him.

After I was back on the street a few days, I met with Tony to talk about the legal mess I was in. He said, "Why don't you change lawyers and hire Oscar [Goodman]? He's a lot sharper than John Momot [my lawyer]."

I didn't think Oscar was doing such a great job for Tony. He kept getting him delays and continuances, but the cases never seemed to get resolved—they kept building up. "Why? Just to prolong the inevitable?"

"Yeah, he can prolong things, but he can win cases, too."

"What case has he ever won for you?"

Tony got pissed. "Look, do you want to listen to me or be a fucking know-it-all?"

I met with Oscar; he wanted $10,000 to represent me. I gave him the money, and he stalled everything. But I was getting in the same boat as Tony—a lot of stuff was hanging over my head and the pressure was building.

* * *

As the days passed I found out more about Sal Romano and his role in the Bertha's fiasco. The Chicago cops had been right about Sal—the FBI had flipped him. They ran a nice operation using Sal to infiltrate us. Even though I didn't warm up to him, Tony and the other guys did and that opened the door. After doing a burglary with Leo and Ernie they'd go to Sal's apartment to cut up the loot. And they did it all on camera, because the apartment was bugged. But they really hit the jackpot when Ernie invited Sal along on Bertha's. When the crew got together at an apartment one last time to go over the plan, Sal Romano was wired and the FBI was parked out on the street listening to every word that was said.

As a result, when we went on the score that night there were about forty FBI agents and cops waiting for us with cameras rolling. They got special radio frequencies assigned that Blasko couldn't pick up on his scanner and even waited to arrest us until Leo actually got inside the store, making it a burglary charge and not just an attempt. Yeah, they set us up beautifully.

There's no doubt that Bertha's was the beginning of the end for us.

20

THE FRIENDSHIP ENDS

Tony was making mistakes he never would have made earlier. Letting his affair with Geri Rosenthal get out of control, running his own operation, and not clearing things through Chicago were very bad news. They were the kinds of things that could land you in jail or in the morgue. I weighed them along with his conduct before and after the Bertha's arrests and didn't like the picture I was seeing. It would soon get worse.

As we learned more and more about how strong the government's Bertha's case was, Tony got very edgy. Even though he hadn't been with us that night, he could be charged by the locals as a conspirator if they could tie him into the plan. And if the feds could show that Tony was part of a criminal organization, they could go after him under RICO. So he had reason to be nervous.

The law didn't let up on us after Bertha's, either—they kept the heat turned on high. When Leo and Ernie got arrested on another burglary beef, I figured I'd be next so I took off for Illinois and hid out on a ranch in Elgin. Sure enough, I got word the cops were looking for me. I called my bondsman in Vegas. He said if I came back and turned myself in I'd probably be able to bond out. I thought about it and figured I had too many charges hanging over my head for the cops to just forget about me. Even if I dodged them on this latest burglary thing, when I didn't show up for court on the other charges they'd be after me and wouldn't rest until they caught me. I decided to go back to Vegas and face the music. The bondsman was right—I made bond. My bonds now totaled over $400,000, and I had more charges hanging over me than I could count.

They say that when it rains, it pours—it did for me. The continuous presence of the cops and FBI around the Upper

Crust had ruined our business, and we had to sell it for $15,000 just to get out from under it. In November of 1981 I was back in jail after getting indicted for possessing furniture stolen in a burglary. I was able to post another bond, but the real bad news was that because of my criminal record, if I got convicted of any of the pending charges they'd put me away for life. The law knew they had the upper hand and put the maximum pressure on everybody.

* * *

I was scheduled to go on trial for the possession of stolen furniture charge in April of 1982. As the court date approached, Elaine started getting bad vibes about Tony and let me know about it. I chalked her attitude up to her being jealous about Tony taking up so much of my time. And then in early April something happened that wasn't so easy for me to dismiss.

We had moved into an apartment next door to Elaine's father. I received a 1:00 a.m. phone call from Tony asking me to meet him in the parking lot of My Place. It wasn't unusual for Tony to want to meet at odd hours so I didn't think much about it at the time.

During the meeting we talked about my upcoming trial and a couple of other things, none of which were urgent. Tony went inside the bar four or five times to use the pay phone. Other than that, there was nothing I considered suspicious.

When I got home Elaine was upset. She said, "What's the matter with that guy? Can't he sleep? Why does he bother you all hours of the day and night? He calls, and you run; this is ridiculous!"

"That's none of your business; don't worry about it."

I had just got into bed when I heard gunshots. I pushed Elaine out of bed onto the floor and then covered her body with mine. When the shooting stopped I went outside to look around. I saw a guy lying in the doorway of the next apartment with blood gushing from a wound in his leg and a van speeding away with the tires squealing. I went back inside and told Elaine the guy next door had been shot, probably due to a drug deal that went sour. She wasn't buying it. "Your friend calls, and you go out to meet him. You get home and aren't in bed two seconds and somebody gets shot next door. *Right next door, Frank!* Come on! Don't you think maybe your friend Tony is trying to kill you?"

I laughed. "You're fucking crazy. You know that, don't you?"

"Laugh all you want, but I've got a feeling Tony wants you dead. I can understand that you're blinded by your friendship for him. But think about what I'm telling you, *please.*"

To shut her up, I said, "Sure, I'll think about it."

My phone rang again about an hour later. It was Tony wanting to know what I was doing and if I could come out for another meeting at the bar. I hung up and said to Elaine, "That was Tony. I'm going back out for a while."

"Frank, he was checking to see if you were dead or alive. Can't you see that? You make sure you tell Tony that I know about the meeting and if anything happens to you, I'll know who was responsible."

I laughed at Elaine for the second time that night and headed out for My Place. I told Tony about the shooting at my apartment building. He said, "Well, imagine that."

I thought his response was a little weird, but that was far from proving Elaine's point. That, however, was about to change.

* * *

April 20, 1982, was a day that changed—and probably saved—my life. It was the day I was convicted in the possession of stolen property case. I didn't have a good feeling about the outcome of the trial from the start. The judge was a pro-prosecution type who kept a .45-caliber handgun between his legs during court. And the prosecutor was too sure of himself. He always had a smug look on his face—like he was holding a pat hand and there was no way I was going to get off. But I had a surprise witness I thought might give me an outside shot at walking.

My lawyer—John Momot—called Elaine's cousin to the stand. He testified that he received the stolen furniture and gave it to me and Elaine. If the jury believed him, I didn't know the stuff was stolen and they'd have to find me not guilty. But they didn't. They returned a guilty verdict in about five hours. The judge refused my request to set an appeal bond, and I was taken straight to jail.

I felt like a deflated balloon. Yet, at the same time, it seemed like a great weight was off my back. Even though I still had other charges hanging over me, I felt a sense of peace. As I sat in my cell I started thinking. I thought about Tony, about the shooting at the apartment next door to mine, and about what Elaine thought. I thought about how messed up everything had gotten in Vegas.

I told Momot to appeal the conviction. He said he'd file an appeal but only if I came up with $10,000. I told him I was almost broke—he'd have to get the money from Tony. When he got back to me, he said Tony was avoiding him and not returning his calls. When he finally caught up with him, Tony said he'd only kick in $6,000; I'd have to come up with the other four.

That got me thinking even more. I'd been doing all the giving, and Tony had been doing all the taking lately. Getting any money out of him for bonds or lawyers was like pulling teeth. I still thought Elaine was full of shit about Tony wanting to kill me. But there was something going on and I didn't like it. I decided I wasn't going to let Tony call the shots for me any longer—I was going to do my own thinking.

Elaine visited me and told me that Herb Blitzstein wanted her to give him her gold cross back. I'd gotten it from the Gold Rush and given it to her as a present. Now, with me behind bars and fighting for my life, the pricks wanted the damn thing back. I was furious. With all the money Tony had—including the hundreds of thousands I'd handed to him over the years—they wanted my wife's gold cross. *Talk about kicking a guy when he's down!*

As unhappy as I was with Tony, he was the only one I could turn to. With the money situation becoming critical, I told Elaine to ask Tony to fix her up with a job. When she did, Tony told her, "Gee, I don't know what I can do for you right now."

And then he offered to find her a job at a restaurant about thirty miles outside of town. Tony was known as the "King of the Strip"—the guy who ran Las Vegas. A waitress job thirty miles away was the best he could do for my wife? *What was I missing?*

Alone in my cell I kept going over everything in my mind. After a while I could no longer escape the reality. Tony had been the Outfit's man in Vegas. He had the world by the balls but had fucked it all up with unauthorized hits, botched robberies, and an affair with Lefty's wife. Tony was on the hook for the Geri Rosenthal business, but it made sense that he'd be looking for a fall guy to lay everything else on. I could almost hear Tony telling the bosses in Chicago, "Frank's out of control and doing his own thing. He's the one hitting people without getting approval. And he brought that fucking rat Sal Romano in on the Bertha's job. I can't control him, and he might bring us all down."

It made sense. Still, I didn't want to believe it and forced those thoughts out of my mind. After all, Tony was having both legal and medical problems and the pressure was probably getting to him a little. He was paranoid and acting a bit weird. He wouldn't sell me out, though—not Tony Spilotro. Not ever.

I made myself believe that until I asked Momot how the appeal was going. He said Tony hadn't paid his share of the fee yet and the appeal hadn't been filed. I told him to get to Tony and get things moving.

When Momot reported back to me he said Tony told him, "There ain't any money available for that now."

Tony had washed his hands of me, and I couldn't make any more excuses for him. The only remaining question was how far he was willing to throw me under the bus. I wasn't sure, but if Elaine was right, I was in a goddamn tough spot.

21

ROLLING

I'd been locked up for ten days when FBI agent Charlie Parsons paid me a visit. On Friday, April 30, 1982, he contacted John Momot and requested a meeting at the jail. I'll never forget Charlie's words that day: "It's been a long week, and I'll be brief. We [the FBI] have a policy that if we become aware that someone's life is in danger, we have to inform that person, regardless of who he is or what we think of him. Frank, we've received credible information that the Chicago Outfit has authorized a contract on your life." He read part of what he said was the transcript of a taped conversation authorizing the hit. "You've been informed. Have a nice weekend."

As soon as Parsons was gone, I said to Momot, *"The motherfuckers are gonna kill me!"*

Momot tried to calm me down. "Take it easy, Frank. They're looking for one of you guys to roll, and they're trying you first. Don't forget, there's nothing in the law that says the FBI can't lie to you. He didn't offer any proof, did he? No, it was just words that anybody could have written."

Momot had a point. But I'd already been thinking that Tony might be tempted to set me up to take some of the pressure off of him. If I got killed, a lot of the stuff Tony was responsible for would end with my death. As far as I was concerned what Parsons said confirmed what I already knew in my heart. I spent a long weekend asking myself: *Is Parsons serious or just bluffing to get me to cooperate?*

By Monday morning I'd made my decision. I called the FBI office and spoke with Parsons. "This is Frank Cullotta. I want to talk to you without my lawyer."

"Don't say anything on the phone. I'll be there in five minutes."

When I met with Parsons on May 3, I wasn't fully committed to becoming a government witness. I thought I could pretend to roll to get a deal and then later recant anything I said. That way I wouldn't put anybody in jail and could keep my reputation as a standup guy.

When Parsons got to the jail he told me he wasn't going to read me my rights. He said he wasn't sure if I really knew anything and wanted to have an off-the-record conversation. First we talked about my lawyer situation. Parsons said, "If we come to an understanding, I suggest you drop John Momot and retain a public defender that would have no ties to other organized crime figures." I said that wouldn't be a problem.

After that Parsons pulled out a yellow legal pad and started asking questions and taking notes. Because this was off-the-record and what I said couldn't be used against me or anybody else, I was pretty open with him about what I could bring to the table. I spoke, and he wrote. Finally, we talked about the Witness Protection Program.

"I've got to be honest with you, Frank. Most people who go into it don't like it, but participation in the program is entirely up to you."

"I know how these people [the Outfit] think and work. If I roll, when they find out they're gonna want to kill me real bad. And if they can't do that, they'll try to intimidate me. I'd want me and my family to go into Witness Protection."

Within a couple of days more agents came to see me. I'd been planning what to say to them when they started asking me things I could be held accountable for or have to testify to. But before they asked me anything they did something that changed everything around. They played a tape their Chicago office had made from a wiretap. It was the conversation Charlie Parsons read to me and Momot when he came to the jail. Only this time it wasn't an FBI agent reading something he could have written himself. I recognized the voices, and it was real.

Tony Spilotro was talking with Joey Lombardo. "I'm telling you, Joey, this fuckin' Frankie is a goddamn maniac. I can't control him any longer, and he's gonna get all of us locked the fuck up."

"I get what you're saying. Take care of your dirty laundry. Understand?"

"I understand."

That was it—all doubts were removed. "Take care of your dirty laundry" was the authorization to kill me. Even though I'd suspected it, hearing those voices I knew so well talking about killing me was still a jolt. My attitude changed on the spot. *Fuck Tony!* I didn't owe him a goddamn thing— or the Outfit, either.

The feds wanted a witness; now they had one. I dropped the idea of lying. Whatever they wanted to know, I'd tell them.

* * *

Even knowing I was on the hit list nobody should think making the decision to become a government witness was easy for me. It was the hardest thing I'd ever done in my life, and I started having regrets after I did it. Not because of some special loyalty to Tony or the Outfit. Loyalty is a two-way street. They'd turned on me and were no longer my friends—all bets were off.

The toughest thing for me was that from the time I was a little kid I'd been taught that a "rat" was the lowest thing you could be. You handled problems yourself and *never ever* went to the law—the law was your enemy.

All my life I'd lived by a code of honor that you never give your friends up to the cops, no matter what. And now I was going against that code. It wasn't just Tony or Outfit guys I'd be giving up. The FBI wanted to know everything

I'd ever done and everything I knew about anybody else—including Leo, Larry, Wayne, and Ernie. I had to weigh that against saving my own life and possibly Elaine's. There was nothing easy about it.

Sitting in my cell after the agents left I thought of one way to save my reputation and take Elaine out of danger: suicide. I'd have gone away without turning rat. And with me gone there'd be no reason to harm Elaine. I considered it for a couple of days and then decided against it. That would have been a coward's way out. I was a lot of things, but a coward wasn't one of them.

* * *

I called John Momot and told him I needed to talk with him at the jail. He'd probably represent some of the people I might have to testify against and—like Parsons said—I needed to get rid of him. When he got to the jail I said, "John, this is the most difficult thing I've ever had to tell anybody in my life. The only other people who know what I'm about to say are with the FBI, so you probably know where I'm coming from. Tony has done me wrong, and I've rolled over. I'm deeply hurt by the way he's treated me and what he's done to me. The worst that can happen to him is some years in prison. I'll either be in jail the rest of my life or take a bullet in my head. Tony has had this all planned. I'd prefer it if you didn't represent me any longer."

Momot seemed shocked. He had tears in his eyes when he asked, "What did they [the cops] do to you? Did they torture you?"

"No, they haven't done anything to me. But Tony has. He deceived me and lied to me and Chicago to protect his own ass. Now he wants me dead. This is the decision I've made, and nothing can possibly change it. There's no turning back for me."

After Momot left I contacted my wife, mother, and

brother. I told each of them what I'd done and why. They had concerns but said they understood and supported my decision.

Elaine told her brother Jerry about me rolling even before Tony Spilotro heard the news. Jerry felt it was in his best interests to let Tony know so he went to My Place and talked with Tony. "I don't know if you've heard about this yet, but Frank's rolled and my sister will be going into Witness Protection."

Jerry told Elaine that Tony laughed so hard he almost fell out of the booth. "You're fucking crazy! Frankie would never do anything like that."

He wouldn't be laughing for long, though.

22

DEBRIEFING

The FBI and Metro wanted to know all about every crime I'd ever committed and crimes I knew my associates had committed or planned. They were especially interested in murders because even if they weren't carried out, the planning could result in conspiracy charges. We talked for days in various locations around Las Vegas, and I gave them the information I had.

They were in shock when I told them about the murders Tony had planned but never gave the final order on. They wanted to know all the details: who the target was, why, and who was going to do the hit. I went through the list for them. I'll go through it again now for you and provide additional background so you'll understand the whats and whys.

<u>Smith & Groover</u>

On the evening of June 9, 1980, Metro detectives Gene Smith and David Groover were in the parking lot outside the Upper Crust in their unmarked police car. They saw a car with Illinois license plates pull in, and that started a series of events that almost started a shooting war between us and the cops.

First I'm going to tell you how the cops explained what happened, and then I'll tell you my side.

According to Smith and Groover, their shift was routine until a 1979 Lincoln with Illinois license plates, pulled into a parking space in front of the Upper Crust. Tony and I were sitting at a table outside the restaurant, and the driver of the Lincoln went inside to order a pizza and then joined us at our table. After we talked for several minutes, the other guy got his pizza and drove away. The cops weren't sure who the guy in the Lincoln was, but because of the Illinois plates and he obviously knew Tony and me, they decided to follow him see what he was up to.

The cops said that as soon as the Lincoln pulled out onto Flamingo Road, the driver started speeding, doing eighty or better, and driving recklessly. With Groover driving, they continued to follow but made no effort to stop the car at that time.

Smith and Groover said that, eventually, they figured there was enough probable cause on the traffic violations to pull the car over and check out the operator. Groover put the red light on the dash, activated it for the driver to pull over, and parked behind him. Groover then exited the vehicle and approached the Lincoln, verbally identifying himself as a police officer and displaying his badge. As he neared the other car, it pulled away at a slow speed, stopping again a short distance away. Groover got back in his car and followed. He again got out and approached the Lincoln. Smith also got out and took up a position by his car's passenger door.

This time, as Groover neared the Lincoln, the driver lowered his window. Groover stated that he again identified himself and displayed his badge. Suddenly Smith hollered, "Watch out, Dave! He's got a gun!"

Groover returned to the police car and stationed himself behind the driver's door, and he and Smith both continued to yell at the driver that they were cops and to put down his gun. They said the driver never said a word, but instead of getting rid of the weapon he turned slightly in his seat, opened his door, and started to get out of the car. The gun was still in his hand and aimed toward Smith. Believing the man was about to shoot, both cops opened fire. Several of the rounds struck the driver. He was rushed to a nearby hospital where he died a couple of hours later. A .22 handgun that had allegedly been in his possession was recovered at the scene.

After the shooting, the cops learned the driver of the Lincoln was Frank Bluestein, a thirty-five-year-old maitre d' at the Hacienda Hotel & Casino, one of the properties controlled by the Chicago Outfit. Also known as Frank

Blue, his father, Steve Bluestein, was an official in the local Culinary Union and had been subject to a 1978 search warrant as part of the FBI's investigation of Tony Spilotro.

Now, here's the story from my side. Tony and I were well aware that Groover and Smith were watching us that night. In fact, we made gestures at them to make sure they knew they'd been spotted. It was a game we played with the cops all the time, and there was nothing unusual about it.

We knew Frank Bluestein through his father, Steve. Frank had moved into town from Chicago a few months earlier and was working in the showroom of the Hacienda. After he ordered his pizza and sat down with us, I said to him, "I see you've still got Illinois plates on your car. Are you going to get a Nevada registration?"

"Someday I will. I just haven't had the time yet."

"You'd better get it done pretty soon. These fuckin' cops here are real cowboys. Any time they see a car with Illinois plates, they think you're a gangster from Chicago."

"You know, I think somebody's been following me around," Bluestein said.

"It's probably the goddamn cops," I told him.

"No, I don't think so; I think it's somebody looking to rob me. Anyway, I've got a gun in the car. If anybody tries anything, I'll be able to take care of myself."

"Do yourself a favor. Get rid of that fucking gun. I'm telling you, these fucking cops are nuts. If they think you've got a gun they'll shoot you."

When his pizza was ready, Frank got up to leave. "Get rid of that piece and get the right plates on your car," I said as he walked away.

About twenty minutes later, my wife came out of the restaurant and told Tony he had an important phone call. Tony went inside and came back out with a shocked look on his face. He said, "That was Herb Blitzstein on the phone; they just killed Frankie Blue."

"Who killed him?"

"The fucking cops," Tony said. "I'm going over there to find out what happened."

"Do you want me to come with you?"

"No, Frankie. Stay here, and I'll be back as soon as I can."

An hour later Tony returned with Herb Blitzstein and Steve Bluestein, and he was in a rage. "The cops claim they tried to get Frankie to get out of his car and that he reached for a gun. That was when they opened up on him. It was Smith and Groover, and they put a lot of bullets into him."

I knew it was Smith and Groover who'd been on us earlier. I considered Smith to be a trigger-happy maniac. Frankie Blue had admitted having a gun in his car, but I wondered whether or not he had actually pulled it on the cops.

Tony said, "We gotta do something with these fucking coppers. I know if we whack one of them, we'll have to fight the Army, Navy, and Marine Corps. You just can't win against these cocksuckers. I gotta figure out a way we can get them corked without it coming back to us. I've gotta think about this, the bastards."

A while later Tony told me his plan. "Frankie, I think I know how we can whack those fucking cops that killed Frank Blue. Do you think your friends in the Blackstone Rangers would give us a hand?"

The Rangers were a black group of stone-cold killers. I'd served time in Illinois with several of them, and we'd become friends. "Yeah. A lot of them are out of prison now and will give me any help I ask for."

"Good. Here's what I want you to do when I'm ready. Get hold of the Rangers and have some of them come here. We'll hit Smith and Groover, but we'll make sure the Rangers are seen in the area. The cops will figure the blacks whacked 'em and come down on them hard. When they go into the Westside [the black neighborhood] looking for suspects, it will be easy for your friends to start a little race war. The cops will have their hands full with the blacks, and we'll be in the clear. What do you think?"

"It sounds okay to me. Just let me know when."

I don't know what happened, but Tony didn't mention it again.

* * *

Ernie Davino

As we entered into the 1980s, me and some of my crew, including Ernie, were becoming annoyed with Tony. One thing that had the guys upset was Tony taking a cut of our scores that he had nothing to do with. Another sore spot was that the law was putting increasing pressure on us—tailing us day and night, arresting us for bullshit traffic violations, and towing our cars. That cost us a lot of money in fines, tows, and increased car insurance rates. And every time we got busted for criminal stuff, there was bail to post and lawyers to pay. Tony, as the boss, should have been helping us out with some of those expenses, especially bail and attorney fees. But he wasn't kicking in anything—he was just taking.

It reached a point where Ernie started making himself scarce. He stopped coming around the regular places and didn't answer his phone. I figured it was because he was unhappy with Tony and the heat from the cops was getting to him. But Tony saw it differently. He suspected that Ernie had become a police informant.

About a week after Ernie dropped out of sight, Tony contacted me. "Have you seen anything of Ernie lately?"

"No, he still hasn't been around."

That seemed to convince Tony that Ernie was a rat. "He's our fuckin' problem. He's talking to the cops."

"Are you sure?"

"Yeah, I'm sure. He's no good; take him out."

I didn't know whether or not Ernie was a snitch. But he was certainly acting funny and maybe Tony was right. But hitting Ernie might be easier said than done. "Jesus, Tony, Ernie's avoiding me; I won't be able to get near him."

"Leo [Guardino] and Ernie are pretty tight. Have Leo set it up for you."

I talked with Leo that night. He didn't believe Ernie was an informant and didn't want any part in setting up the hit. I told him I understood and that I'd get somebody else.

I reached out to Larry Neumann. His response was, "I'll be glad to do it; I never liked that asshole anyway. How do you want him killed?"

"It's your job and your call."

"Okay. I think I'll cut him into little pieces and throw him in Lake Mead."

I wasn't into that kind of stuff, but it was Larry's hit and I wasn't going to tell him how to do it. "Like I said, that's up to you. If you need some help, Jimmy Patrazzo [a thief and killer from Chicago] is in town. Take him with you."

Larry came up with a plan to ask Ernie to go with him and Patrazzo to check out a score; when they got him to a vacant house they'd kill him

But it turned out that Larry wasn't able to make contact with Ernie, either. When I told Tony, he said, "I'll get in touch with the cocksucker. If I can get him to my house, I know I can make him feel comfortable and he'll start coming around again." Tony's plan worked. He lured Ernie out, and he started making himself available.

I told Larry that Ernie was starting to relax and he'd probably be able to get to him. He contacted Ernie and made arrangements to meet a week later to check on the fictitious burglary. But before that meeting took place, Tony called off the hit. He said, "I found out Ernie's not the culprit. Pass on it."

I was happy that Ernie was off the hook, but Larry was another story. "I've got everything ready, and I've already put 500 bucks into it. Fuck Tony. Ernie's an asshole, and I'm going to kill him anyway." After a long talk, I was able to calm Larry down.

By avoiding us for as long as he did, Ernie saved his own life. He bought himself enough time for Tony to change his mind and cancel the hit. And I'm glad it worked out that way.

* * *

Lefty

Tony took in quite a bit of tribute money from renegade bookies, and every so often he'd send me to Chicago to give the bosses their share. I'd just returned to Vegas from a money run when Tony said he wanted to see me.

"I've got a job I might need to have done," he said. "I want you to prepare for it. Make sure Larry [Neumann] is ready to go and get one other guy. Who else can you get?"

"What's the job?"

"I might want to get rid of the Jew [Rosenthal]."

I wasn't surprised. The relationship between Tony and Lefty had long since deteriorated past the point of no return.

"For something like that, I can have Wayne come in from Chicago."

"I'm not sure right now I want to do this, so don't do anything until I tell you. I'm going to bring in a couple of other guys, one from California [no doubt Joey Hansen] and the other from Arizona. They're going to dig a big hole in the desert. They'll cover it with plywood and dirt. You'll know where the hole is because I'll take you there and show you. When I'm ready to get rid of the Jew, I'll tell you. Then you scoop him up from the street. Don't kill him on the street, Frankie. Kill him when you get to the grave we're going to dig. Then dump him in and cover him up. That will be the end of it."

I had no problem with whacking Lefty. The only question in my mind was whether Tony would seek permission from Chicago to take Rosenthal out or make the decision on his own, as he had apparently done in the Lisner killing.

I worked for Tony, not the Outfit. If he gave me the order to kill Rosenthal, I'd have done it and worried about the consequences later. But the planned hit never went any further. Looking back on it now, though, I don't believe the idea of killing Lefty was just a personal thing for Tony. I think Kansas City had approached the Outfit with their concerns about Lefty, and the bosses told Tony to be ready. After thinking it over Chicago decided against it, and a few months later Kansas City made their own attempt on Lefty with the car bomb.

* * *

Sal Romano & Joe Blasko

On July 4, 1981, me and my crew were busted during the burglary of Bertha's Gifts and Home Furnishings on East Sahara. We had walked into a trap run by the FBI and Las Vegas Metro, and it was set up by an informant who had infiltrated us named Sal Romano. I had tried to talk Tony out of using Romano or former cop Joe Blasko, but he insisted they were okay. I didn't trust Blasko just because he had been a cop. There was something about Romano that told me he was bad news, and I even heard from a couple of Chicago cops that he might be a snitch. I couldn't convince Tony, though, and he was the boss.

After I and the rest of the guys made bail, Tony told me that two men needed to be killed: Joe Blasko and Sal Romano.

"The Big Guy [Blasko] is getting me nervous," Tony said.

"Why? What's he doing?"

"He's sort of insinuating that I didn't listen to you guys about Romano. Couldn't I feel a problem coming on with the guy? And why did I let him in on the score? Stuff like that. I'm afraid the motherfucker is going to roll on me, Frankie.

I want you to get rid of him."

As far as I was concerned, it was a case of better late than never. But Tony later backed off on the hit, saying Blasko was behaving himself and to let it go.

He had no sympathy on Romano, though, and insisted he had to go.

I said, "I'd love to kill that son of a bitch, Tony. But how in the fuck are we going to get to him? He's in Witness Protection being guarded by the U.S. Marshals."

"I don't know where they've got Sal stashed, but they'll have to bring him into town to testify, and when they do, we can get him."

"I still don't see how we're going to know where he is."

"I know the guy that caters food to the marshals when they're protecting someone. When they bring Sal here, they'll have to feed him. I'll be able to find out where the food is delivered to, and then we can whack him."

"But he'll have a lot of guys around guarding him. What about them?"

Tony said, "You gotta do what you gotta do if you want to stay free. Hit them, all of them. That's it—an open and shut case."

This plan never got past the talking stage either. Tony was making plans to have a lot of people whacked but seemed unable to issue the final orders.

* * *

Me

I told the G and the cops that as kind of a joke. But in reality it was true. I am the last guy I know for sure that Tony wanted killed. As I said, when the FBI played that tape of Joey Lombardo authorizing my murder, my loyalty to Tony was over. Had I not rolled I would have been dead very soon, but that wouldn't have saved Tony's life, at least not for very long. He'd already burned too many bridges with the guys in Chicago, and it was just a matter of time before they took him out.

23

FACING THE MUSIC

The government tried to keep my cooperation quiet for as long as possible, but I'm sure the word leaked out in the Las Vegas underworld. The media and the general public were unaware of it for a while, though, and then the whole thing came out during a court proceeding that I didn't participate in directly.

The law wanted to get Larry Neumann off the streets real bad, and I was giving up a lot of information on him—things that could put him away for a long, long time. The trouble was it would take time to verify everything I was saying. Knowing that if Larry remained free he posed a threat to potential witnesses, they had to come up with a way to lock him up until they were ready to move on my stuff.

The only thing they had against Larry at the time was a 1981 arrest as an ex-felon in possession of a concealed weapon, for which he was out on bail. They got that case into court, and Larry was convicted and sentenced to two years. His lawyer immediately filed a motion to get him out on bond while the conviction was appealed.

At the subsequent bail hearing prosecutors had to demonstrate that Larry presented a danger if he was released and his request for bond should be denied. As part of their presentation Charlie Parsons testified that at one time Larry planned to kill Ernie Davino and that I was the source of the information. I wasn't there, but I understand a gasp went up from the spectators in the courtroom. The word was out.

The Vegas papers treated the news as a major event. The *Review-Journal* and *Las Vegas Sun* both speculated about how much damage my cooperation with prosecutors would do to the Mob, in general, and Tony Spilotro, in particular. Their stories said the information I was providing would blow the lid off Tony's street crime rackets.

Although rumors had been circulating on the streets that I had defected, the newspaper articles provided confirmation. I heard that those articles caused tremors in the criminal underworld all the way to Chicago.

* * *

I learned pretty quickly that my original plan to lie to the law wouldn't have worked. I was made to understand right up front that my deal was based on telling the truth. The FBI and Metro didn't want to hear any lies or embellishments— only things that I knew for sure. There was a lot of paperwork, and I had to be evaluated and take psychological tests and a polygraph. I was impressed with how much you had to go through to get into the program. You had to prove your honesty and value to them first. And if they ever caught you in a lie, the deal was off.

One of the ways they verified my honesty was by matching police reports with my descriptions of crimes. So when I gave them the date and location of a burglary and the items taken, my statement was compared with police incident reports on file. And then they'd take me past the site of the burglary and have me identify the specific house.

While I was being debriefed by Metro and the FBI, my assigned lawyer negotiated with federal and local prosecutors to get me the best deal possible to resolve all pending charges against me plus, of course, immunity from charges for any additional crimes I would testify to.

On July 8, 1982, my plea arrangement was finalized and I appeared in court for sentencing. The local papers ran stories, and the headline in the *Las Vegas Review-Journal* was "Cullotta gets eight-year prison term." The reporter described the security in and around the courthouse as "heavy," and I agree. The courtroom was loaded with FBI agents and Metro cops—I counted seven. They searched everybody who entered the courtroom. And there were two more stationed on the roof.

District Judge Paul Goldman sentenced me to the eight years that had been agreed upon. It had further been agreed that although my sentence would be to a state prison, I'd serve my time in a federal facility.

* * *

With my sentencing out of the way, I had to face the really difficult part of my decision to cooperate with the government: facing my former friends and associates in court. I knew they and their lawyers would be coming after me with everything they had, both inside and outside the courtroom. I couldn't let them tempt me with offers of money for me or my family, and I had to keep my temper under control while the lawyers tried to destroy me on the stand.

However, my first courtroom testimony for the government was not to get a conviction. It was to provide character evidence at a pre-sentencing hearing in Chicago on February 8, 1983. The defendant was my old Outfit buddy Joey "the Clown" Lombardo. Joey had been convicted of bribery and was facing up to fifty-five years in prison. Prosecutors wanted me to tell what I knew about his ties to the Outfit and his position within the organization.

On the eighth of February I went into the heavily guarded courtroom and gave my testimony.

I told the jury I had once sought permission from Lombardo to kill a man for causing a problem at my disco. Lombardo nixed the killing but said I could break the guy's hands and legs.

I repeated exactly what Lombardo had told me: "What I want you to do is break his hands, break his legs. Then if he don't get the message, later on you can kill him."

My testimony helped the government make its case that Lombardo was a powerful mobster who could decide matters of life and death.

Then I had to tell all about my criminal career that dated back to my days as a teenager. I admitted doing twenty-five arsons, fifty armed robberies, and 200 burglaries. I also admitted participating in two murders and arranging two others.

In spite of my record, the jurors apparently believed me and sentenced Lombardo to fifteen years.

* * *

Now that I was actively testifying, some of my associates started getting nervous—including Tony. He knew I'd be a primary witness against him in the future, and his brother Michael reached out to me through my brother. He said, "Tell your brother not to testify against Tony, and we'll give you enough money to fill a good-size house." I sent word back to him that I wasn't interested.

When that failed the Spilotros tried to intimidate me. They said if I testified, Tony's lawyers would subpoena my mother as a defense witness. That threat never came off, though. I suspect they thought it over and decided having my mother testify against me could backfire and turn into a public-relations disaster. Their bribe and intimidation tactics didn't work, but the death threat was still hanging over my head and I knew that was the solution they'd prefer.

* * *

Coming face-to-face with my former friends who I was helping to get locked up wasn't easy, and there were four trials in particular that had the greatest impact on me. There were two in which Larry Neumann was tried for killing the Chicago jeweler Bob Brown and two involving Tony Spilotro: the M&M Murders and the Bertha's trial.

I'll talk about Larry first. He was indicted for Brown's

murder based mostly on my grand-jury testimony. He was tried twice for that killing, and I testified at both. The first trial ended in a hung jury. The second resulted in a conviction and a sentence of life in prison without the possibility of parole.

I remember being escorted into court and having to walk past the holding cell Larry was in. One of my guards hollered at Larry, "Turn your back."

Larry yelled back, "Fuck you, you cocksuckers! I know who you've got there."

Larry didn't say anything to me directly as I passed by the cell, but our eyes met for a moment. My impression was that he couldn't believe what I was doing to him. It was a very uncomfortable few seconds.

Larry died in prison on January 9, 2007, of cardiac disease at the age of seventy-eight. His unclaimed body was cremated.

Now for Tony. Here I'll tell you about the M&M trial and in the next chapter I'll get into the Bertha's trial in detail. Before I begin, let me say that in each of my court appearances against Tony he never spoke to me or even looked at me—we never made eye contact. Also, the only family member of Tony's that I ever saw in the courtroom was his wife, Nancy.

In January 1983, Tony was indicted in Cook County, Illinois, for the 1962 murders of James Miraglia and William McCarthy—the so-called M&M Murders. Chicago Mayor Richard Daley announced the indictment during a press conference and said it was based primarily on my grand-jury testimony. Following the press conference, Tony was arrested in Las Vegas and jailed to await extradition to Illinois.

Oscar Goodman and Tony's regular Chicago lawyer, Herb Barsy, teamed up to defend Tony when the case went to trial. Barsy was known as a guy who knew how to work the system and get things done. He proved his reputation was well-earned.

I knew going in that getting a guilty verdict in a twenty-one-year-old case would be tough. But I started to really doubt we'd get a conviction when Judge Thomas J. Maloney was assigned to hear the case. I'd heard that Maloney was a guy that could be dealt with, and after the offer made to me by Michael Spilotro I knew Tony was ready to deal. And then the second shoe dropped when it was announced that Tony was going to forego a jury trial and let Maloney decide his fate. *What?*

At a jury trial there are twelve people you can potentially sway or bribe to get a hung jury or an acquittal. This was a double-murder case, so why would you want to put all your eggs in one basket? In my mind there was only one reason: they'd gotten to Maloney.

And sure enough, when the trial ended Judge Maloney ruled that the prosecution hadn't proved its case beyond a reasonable doubt and Tony walked.

Now here's the rest of the story. In 1993, ten years after the M&M trial, Judge Maloney became the only Illinois judge ever convicted of fixing a murder case. Maloney got caught up in two big federal investigations of corruption in the Chicago courts. As a result of Operation Greylord and Operation Gambat, ninety-two people, including defense attorneys, bailiffs, clerks, and thirteen judges, were indicted. One of those thirteen was Maloney. He was convicted in 1993 on charges of racketeering conspiracy, extortion under color of official right, and obstruction of justice. Those charges came from three cases in which he took bribes. In 1994 he was sentenced to fifteen years in prison and fined $200,000.

Even though those charges weren't specific to Tony's case, do I think his trial was fixed? You bet your life!

Tony may have gotten away for the M&M Murders, but he couldn't celebrate for long. Just a few months later he was indicted again, this time for racketeering as part of the Bertha's case.

24

THE TRIAL

There is a book out there that claims Tony had been acquitted in the first Bertha's trial in Chicago and was awaiting retrial in Las Vegas when he was killed. That account is bogus in two important respects: first, if a defendant is acquitted there is no retrial; and second, that trial was held in Las Vegas, not Chicago.

I'll tell you the inside story of the Bertha's trial in a second, but first I need to set the stage.

When the feds learned of the skim they began investigations of the casino operations and, along with Las Vegas Metro, Tony's street crimes. They were determined to put the Mob out of business. They got the skimmers first.

On September 30, 1983, a federal grand jury in Kansas City returned an eight-count indictment against fifteen defendants in the Argent case, including Tony Spilotro, whose case was severed from the other defendants. The trial started in late 1985, and in January 1986 the Outfit's Joey Aiuppa, Jackie Cerone, and Joey Lombardo were among those convicted. Aiuppa and Cerone each received sentences totaling twenty-eight and a half years. Lombardo drew sixteen years. In addition, each man was fined $80,000.

There are two important points here regarding Tony. His case was severed from the others. Those charges continued to hang over his head, making him more susceptible to accepting a deal with the government that would require him to tell what he knew about his associates—and he knew plenty. In addition, the Mob's piggy bank was gone and several top mobsters were in prison. Everybody was pissed off and there were a lot of fingers being pointed. Some of them were directed at Tony Spilotro and Lefty Rosenthal— the two guys who were supposed to make sure nothing like this happened. Tony was in deep trouble with the Mob even before the Bertha's trial began.

* * *

The defendants in the Bertha's trial were all indicted on racketeering charges by a federal grand jury in 1983, based in large part on my testimony. The counts against them included armed robbery, extortion, and transporting stolen property across state lines. Tony had the most counts because, as the boss, he was responsible for the actions of everyone under him. His co-defendants were his brother Michael, Ernie Davino, Leo Guardino, Herb Blitzstein, Wayne Matecki, Pete Basile, Larry Neumann, Joe Blasko, and Mitch Manis. There were two other defendants who were peripheral players, Earnest Lehning and Fred Pandalfo.

The trial was originally scheduled to begin in Las Vegas in May of 1985, but it was continued a couple of times because Tony was also a defendant in another case being tried in Kansas City and the trial dates conflicted. The Vegas trial was moved back to November and then postponed again because Tony developed heart problems and had by-pass surgery in Houston, Texas, in August and was severed from the Kansas City case. His doctor, Michael DeBakey, said Tony suffered from congestive heart failure and would not be able to go on trial in Las Vegas in November.

The court ordered an independent medical exam, which took place in San Francisco. The cardiologist agreed that Tony needed a little more time but said he should be fine by early 1986.

Finally, on January 14, 1986, jury selection began in Las Vegas, and it was a big story locally. Lawrence "Larry" Leavitt was the lead government prosecutor and was assisted by Strike Force attorney Stan Parry. Larry graciously agreed to be interviewed by Denny Griffin as part of the research for this book. Any of Larry's comments from that interview used in the balance of this chapter will appear in quotes.

Tony was still complaining of heart problems. One day during jury selection his face turned a bright red, and because he was free on bail, he left the courtroom, obviously not feeling well. Larry Leavitt recalled that incident:

"He [Tony] went to the clerk's office, where he was given water and sat for a while. When he returned to the courtroom a half hour or so later, he looked fine. There were no other health-related incidents during the course of the proceedings."

Larry also remembered some of the other things about this trial that were out of the ordinary.

"Due to the high-profile nature of the trial, the judge ordered that an exceptionally large number of prospective jurors—about five times the number for an ordinary trial—be called, and also increased the number of U.S. Marshals who would be in the courtroom.

"Throughout the trial, whenever the defendants were in the courtroom, several marshals stood nearby with stun guns concealed under their clothing should any of the accused get out of line.

"During jury selection, the candidates were examined individually in the courtroom with none of the other prospective jurors present. After two weeks we were able to seat twelve jurors and, in anticipation of a lengthy trial, six alternates.

"There are a couple of things that happened prior to trial that need to be mentioned. One of which may very well have eliminated the need to have a trial at all.

"The first was an effort to reach a plea agreement with Tony. None of his co-defendants were anxious to testify against him and knew any deal offered to them would involve them having to incriminate him. So they all held fast. Had Tony made a deal it would more than likely have had a domino effect and everyone else would have pled out.

"In the late fall of 1985, Oscar's [Tony's attorney Oscar Goodman] partner Steve Stein called me to discuss a possible plea deal for Tony. We had a series of conversations, but a deal never came to fruition because I wouldn't accept as soft a sentence as Steve wanted.

"His first offer was for Tony to do five years. I rejected that.

"Steve then said that a seven-and-a-half year sentence might be acceptable and later indicated Tony might agree to do ten years. We were getting closer, but I said I wouldn't sign off on any sentence of less than fifteen years. And the only reason I was willing to go that low was because the indictment didn't include any murders. Tony wouldn't go for it, and that was the end of negotiations.

"The other thing worthy of mention is that prior to trial, we moved to disqualify Oscar Goodman from representing Tony. The stated reason for the disqualification was the fact that Oscar had previously represented Frank Cullotta, who was going to be a key government witness. It was our position that it would be impossible for Oscar to cross-examine Cullotta without getting into attorney-client confidentiality issues from the prior representation.

"At the pre-trial hearing the judge ruled that rather than completely disqualify Oscar, he would not be allowed to cross-examine Cullotta. Oscar brought in a lawyer named McKenzie from Chicago to handle Cullotta, and the issue was resolved."

* * *

With the jury empanelled and any necessary legal issues decided, the presentation of evidence began. Larry Leavitt described the atmosphere this way:

"There was definitely excitement in the air, and the

courtroom was packed every single day with media and spectators, along with the twelve defendants—each of whom had his own lawyer—the prosecution team, and court staff.

"Because of the number of defendants and lawyers, the courtroom had to be reconfigured. Several large tables were brought in and placed in a squared-off letter U shape with the points extending to near the clerk's station, just in front of the judge's bench.

"As it worked out, Larry Neumann, whom I thought was the most deranged and violent of all the defendants, and his lawyer were sitting about three feet from the lectern where the lawyers stood when examining witnesses. Knowing he was that close was slightly unnerving at first, but I didn't think he was deranged enough to try anything and there were enough marshals around to stop him if he did.

"The prosecution went first of course, and our strategy was pretty straightforward. We spent the first several days putting on a series of victims who had been robbed or extorted, to get their stories on the table and put faces to the crimes. Those witnesses proved to be very effective, with one exception.

"A woman testified she'd had several items of jewelry stolen, including a valuable ring, and filed an insurance claim against her loss. Her testimony was directly related to the charges against Herb Blitzstein. However, it was learned during the course of the trial that the ring was not stolen, and she had filed a false insurance claim.

"When it came to light that she had offered perjured testimony, there was no choice but to have the charges against Blitzstein dismissed and remove him from the case."

* * *

After the testimony of the victims, the prosecution put on its two key witnesses: me and Sal Romano. Larry described us as "interesting characters" and remembered Sal this way:

"Sal was a thief out of Chicago and knew several of the defendants, including Tony, Basile, and Neumann. He also knew Frank Cullotta. When things got too hot for Sal in Chicago he relocated to Tucson, Arizona, with his teenage son, where they started robbing the coin boxes from washers and dryers in laundromats and the laundry rooms in apartment complexes.

"The local police began placing cameras in various facilities and got lucky. Sal and his son entered one of the laundry rooms being monitored, and the police busted the pair when they walked out with the loot.

"When the Tucson police interrogated Sal, they learned of his Chicago ties and possible connections to some organized crime figures. Tucson called the FBI to see if they had an interest in talking with Sal. They did.

"An agent met with Sal, and a very productive relationship developed. Sal didn't want his son to face the consequences of their crime spree. So he told the agent that if his son got a pass, he'd cooperate. The deal was made, and Sal in effect became an undercover FBI informant. His first assignment was to move to Las Vegas and infiltrate Tony Spilotro's crew, known as the Hole in the Wall Gang.

"The FBI set up an elaborate cover for Sal, including renting an apartment for him that was set up with audio and video recording equipment, providing him a car with an audio recording device, and having a female agent play the role of his girlfriend on occasion.

"Sal was able to gain the confidence of Tony and several of his crew. The only guy who didn't seem to take to him was Frank Cullotta. In spite of Frank's reservations about him, Sal began to go on burglaries with some of the crew and recorded them when they met at his apartment to discuss a score or at meetings elsewhere when he was wearing a wire.

"The information Sal developed led to a joint FBI and Las Vegas Metropolitan Police operation that ended on July 4,

1981, with the arrest of Cullotta and five other crew members during the commission of a burglary at an upscale jewelry and home furnishing store named Bertha's. Following the arrests Sal entered the federal Witness Protection Program.

"Without Sal there would have been no arrests at Bertha's and virtually no chance of obtaining Frank Cullotta's cooperation.

"I was quite sure there was no love lost between Sal and Frank, so when Sal testified Frank wasn't in the courthouse. In fact, he wasn't even in Las Vegas.

"Sal was on the stand for nearly a week and did beautifully. The recordings of his conversations with the crew members that we played spoke for themselves and corroborated his testimony. I couldn't have been happier."

Larry knew what he was doing when he kept me away from Sal. I thought of Sal as just a petty thief—robbing laundry machines wasn't exactly major crime—and felt all along that he was a fucking rat—I hadn't been able to convince Tony of it, though.

* * *

Larry then recalled his dealings with me:

"In the second huge turning point in the investigation, not long after the Bertha's incident, Frank and Tony had a falling out and Tony asked Chicago for permission to kill Frank. The FBI recorded a conversation between Tony and his boss in Chicago, Joey Lombardo, during which the request was made and the permission given. In April 1982 they played that tape for Frank, and in a matter of days he decided to flip. He became a government witness and soon thereafter testified in Chicago against some of his former associates.

"As I got ready for trial I realized that Frank had a lot of baggage. In addition to his own criminal record, I had read the transcripts of his previous testimony in Chicago. His cross-examinations were a disaster. I didn't necessarily blame Frank for that. I felt it was a case of the prosecution not properly preparing him, and the defense lawyers were able to provoke him and get him to lose his temper.

"I spent countless hours working with Frank before the trial and was confident he'd be able to hold up, no matter what the defense lawyers threw at him.

"Frank followed Sal on the stand as the second half of my one-two punch. He was especially important because his role with Tony put him in a position to testify that Tony was the leader of a criminal organization, that he ordered and helped plan criminal activities, and that he profited from them.

"However, unlike with Sal, there were no recordings to corroborate Frank's testimony. Once he took the stand he'd have to stay composed and come across as believable.

"Frank also testified for a week and did a remarkable job. On my direct examination he made every point that needed to be made and was completely credible. In fact, he was so compelling that during a break after I concluded my direct, some of the lawyers who had been involved when Frank testified earlier in Chicago, told me they were amazed at the difference in him.

"On cross-examination Frank only lost his cool once when a defense lawyer attacked his mother, trying to implicate her in some wrongdoing. Frank expressed his displeasure, and I think it came across to the jury as an authentic and justified reaction.

"Like I said, it was a remarkable performance under extremely stressful conditions."

* * *

I have one thing to add to Larry's account. Prior to the start of the trial I was locked up in the witness protection unit of the federal prison in San Diego. Not long before I was scheduled to testify I was removed from general population and placed in isolation without explanation. After a few days I was taken back to my tier and noticed one of the other inmates was gone. Since we were all witnesses I figured he was probably testifying in court somewhere. It turned out he had been removed in regard to his testimony—he was going to testify against me at the Bertha's trial.

As I learned later, the guy was a regular jailhouse snitch. He knew about Tony's upcoming trial and that I'd be a star witness for the government. He reached out to Oscar Goodman on the jail pay phone and offered to discredit me on the stand. Whether he realized it or not, all those calls were recorded and the government knew what was coming, but they didn't tell me what was going on. They removed me from the tier until they could relocate the snitch and then brought me back. I was really shocked when he showed up in Vegas as a defense witness.

To counter his testimony of what a bad guy I was, the prosecutors called two of the prison guards from my tier and a guy from the Witness Protection Program who had evaluated me for acceptance into the program. They testified that I was totally honest and credible during the screening process and that I was a model inmate while locked up. One of the guards even said that if he met me on the street he wouldn't hesitate to invite me over to his house for dinner.

The snitch was the one who got discredited.

* * *

After both sides rested, the defense lawyers each made motions to have the charges against their client dismissed due to insufficient evidence to warrant conviction. The judge granted those motions regarding Michael Spilotro and Fred Pandalfo, and they were removed from the case.

Larry told me he'd felt all along that the cases against

them were weak and they probably shouldn't have been indicted to begin with, so he took no issue with the judge's ruling.

The jury began their deliberations in the nine remaining cases on March 27, 1986, at which point they were sequestered. Larry Leavitt and all of us on the prosecution side could do nothing but wait and wonder as the days passed without a verdict.

Larry recalled the waiting this way:

"They [the jurors] were put up in rooms at the Hacienda Hotel and Casino [now the site of Mandalay Bay] at the south end of the Strip. U.S. Marshals provided their security and transported them by bus to and from the courthouse, where they deliberated.

"It has been my experience that the most stressful time in a case is when it's in the hands of the jury, and that was certainly true this time. After physically and mentally exhausting myself for several months, twelve strangers were now going to have the final say.

"Even knowing the jurors were dealing with nine defendants and multiple counts didn't prevent the angst I felt as the days passed. A couple of times they submitted written questions to the judge and all the lawyers were summoned to the courtroom to discuss how to respond to the issue involved. When an agreement was reached the jury was called in and the judge read them the answer we'd agreed on. And then it was back to preparing for other cases and waiting for a resolution to that one.

"On April 8, the eleventh day of deliberations, we were called to the courtroom regarding a letter the judge received from one of the jurors. The gist of the letter was that the female juror felt there were two male jurors who might have been improperly influenced. I knew this could be serious, and my heart went into my throat.

"The judge called the author of the letter into the

courtroom and had her take the witness stand. He asked her to describe in more detail why she was concerned about the two male jurors.

"She said that within the first few days of deliberations the two men basically shut down and withdrew from the process. They seemed to have already made up their minds that they were not going to vote to convict anybody, especially Tony Spilotro, based on the testimony of Frank Cullotta and Sal Romano, and they were not actively participating in the discussions.

"The woman said that just the previous day as the jurors returned to the hotel and walked up the stairs to their rooms, she was walking directly behind the two men. They were talking to each other in low voices, and she heard one of them mention $10,000. That, in conjunction with their attitudes, made her very suspicious that someone had gotten to them. She didn't know what to do so she wrote the letter to the judge.

"At this point the judge asked her the sixty-four-dollar question. 'Do you believe that under these circumstances, you and the jury can continue to deliberate in a good faith effort to reach a verdict in regard to all of the defendants?'

"I held my breath. 'No, I don't believe we can,' she answered.

"With that, the judge declared a mistrial. The retrial was scheduled to begin on June 23.

"Following a mistrial being declared, I asked the FBI to investigate and find out if the jury had in fact been tampered with. They approached the two male jurors in question, read them their rights, and asked them if they'd consent to a polygraph exam. Both men were understandably offended about being suspected of being on the take and made their feelings clear.

"While the agents were discussing the situation with them one of the agents raised the conversation in which $10,000 had been mentioned. That seemed to generate an understanding in the men of what might have happened.

"They explained that the stairs they took at the hotel had glass walls on both sides, one of which overlooked the parking lot. The conversation about the money concerned a yellow Corvette they observed in the parking lot that was owned by one of the marshals serving on their transport team. The marshal had mentioned she owned the Corvette and would sell it for $10,000. That's what they had been talking about.

"The agents interviewed the marshal, and she confirmed the story. That was the end of the investigation.

"On June 16, a week before the retrial was to begin, Tony was reported missing. The bodies of Tony and his brother Michael were found a few days later buried in a cornfield in Indiana. They were apparently the victims of the Mob, a fact that was confirmed during the Family Secrets trial in Chicago in 2007.

"After Tony's death the floodgates opened, and the other eight defendants became interested in making deals. Their lawyers contacted me to negotiate, and we reached agreements with all of them. Their clients received sentences ranging from two to eight years. Larry Neumann got only two years, but he was already serving a sentence for murder of life without parole in Illinois.

"The skim operations at the casinos had previously been successfully prosecuted, and now the street crimes had been dealt with. The Chicago Outfit's reign in Las Vegas was over."

25

THE DEATH OF TONY SPILOTRO

While waiting for Tony's retrial to begin, the U.S Marshals put me up in a motel in an undisclosed location. I was in my room when I received a message to call the FBI. Agent Dennis Arnoldy, who was my handler and debriefer, wanted to talk with me. He said, "Tony and Michael Spilotro have disappeared. Have you got any idea where they would have run to?"

I answered right away. "They haven't run. Tony would never run. He fucked up, and he's dead. If his brother is with him, he's dead, too."

"What makes you so sure?"

"Tony's caused the Outfit a lot of problems, and he stopped generating money. Michael is cocky and has caused problems, too. They aren't needed, anymore. If you whack one, you've gotta whack them both. I guarantee you they're both dead."

I was right. On Tuesday, June 24, 1986, the *Las Vegas Review-Journal* ran a front-page story confirming Tony's death. It said Tony and Michael were reported missing on June 16 by Michael's wife, Anne. She last saw them June 14 at their house in Oak Park, Illinois. Several days later a farmer discovered the two badly beaten bodies in a shallow grave in his Indiana cornfield. The bodies were positively identified as Tony and Michael.

According to the Indiana State Police, the bodies were only wearing underwear and were buried one on top of the other in a five-foot grave. They were apparently killed by blunt-force injuries, probably caused by hands or feet.

The grave was about five miles from a farm owned by Outfit boss Joey Aiuppa, who had been convicted three months earlier for skimming money from Las Vegas casinos. It was unknown if there was any connection between Aiuppa and the murders.

What bothered me the most was the way they were killed. During another phone call with Arnoldy, I told him, "The way Tony and Michael were killed was terrible. They were beaten to death! Not shot. No cut throats. They were beaten—beaten to death. That's a hell of a way to die. Even though Tony wanted me dead, nobody should go like that. That was the Outfit's way of showing that Tony wasn't that tough a guy."

Arnoldy asked, "Have you got any idea why they were buried the way they were?"

"The Outfit didn't intend for the bodies to be discovered so soon; they weren't looking for any more heat. The bodies were buried okay; no mistakes were made there. It was just that the farmer knew his land too well and spotted the fresh dig."

* * *

There was a lot of media interest in the murders, and for the next several weeks more information was printed. Some of it was fact, and the rest was speculation. Kent Clifford, the head of Las Vegas Metro's Intelligence Bureau, said, "Tony's ego and his ambitions caused most of his problems with the Mob. By us and the FBI keeping him in the news, he became too much of a liability. Either the law was going to put him away or the Mob would take care of him. For Spilotro, those were the only two possible outcomes."

Lieutenant Gene Smith, who worked for Clifford, said, "The department had been receiving intelligence that Tony's days were numbered. He'd been falling out of favor with the bosses for quite a while because he wouldn't give up his street rackets and keep a low profile. But he was real tight with Joe Lombardo and that probably extended his life. When Lombardo and the others went to prison on the Strawman [casino skim] convictions, Tony lost his protection. He wasn't liked or trusted by the new regime, and that sealed his fate. It was just a matter of when.

"As for Michael, the word was that he was running a protection racket in Chicago without the approval of the Outfit and not cutting them in on the profits. There was also the possibility that if they only hit Tony, Michael might want revenge. The best solution for the boys in Chicago was to get rid of both of them at the same time."

Clifford and Smith were right; Tony had infuriated the Chicago bosses by his behavior in Vegas. His conduct had contributed to their cash flow from the skim coming to an end and a lot of guys going to prison. Tony was in trouble, and he had to know it. So why would he voluntarily agree to meet with his potential killers?

A popular scenario at the time—and alluded to later during court proceedings—was that Tony went to Chicago because Michael was going to become a made man and wanted him there. I don't buy it, though. Tony wouldn't have believed that story—he would have sensed a trap.

Smith was also right about Michael; he was having his own problems with the Outfit and Joe Ferriola, the current boss, couldn't stand him. Ferriola told me how much he disliked Michael before I moved to Las Vegas, but I never told Tony because of the problems it would have caused. And later, during one of my money runs to Chicago, Ferriola told me directly, "If it weren't for his brother [Tony], Michael would have been dead a long time ago."

They say that blood is thicker than water, and under those circumstances Tony would have had no choice but to go or he wouldn't have been able to live with himself. I believe in my heart that because of that Tony was willing to take a risk. He went to that meeting because he wanted a sit down with the bosses to try to straighten things out for Michael and prevent him from getting whacked.

Whatever the reason, Tony agreed to make the trip and the get-together was scheduled for June 14 two days before the start of the second Bertha's trial in Las Vegas. He and Michael left Michael's house for the meeting that day and got whacked by the Outfit. Their bodies were found in that cornfield, but I never thought they were killed there—the Outfit wouldn't have done it that way. I was pretty sure they were probably whacked in a building or the cellar of a house. I didn't figure the murders would ever be solved and wasn't even sure how hard the law would try to identify the killers. It turned out I was wrong about a lack of effort.

* * *

On April 25, 2005, almost nineteen years after the Spilotro brothers were murdered, the Department of Justice issued a press release announcing indictments resulting from a lengthy FBI investigation called Operation Family Secrets. As soon as I got the call telling me about the release, I went to the DOJ site and read it for myself. Using the RICO statute, they'd charged fourteen Outfit guys with a bunch of racketeering stuff, including eighteen unsolved murders. Among them were Tony and Michael.

The release said seven of the defendants had committed or agreed to commit murders on behalf of the Outfit. The arrestees included Outfit bigwigs James Marcello, Joseph Lombardo, Michael Marcello, hit man Frank Schweihs, and Anthony Doyle. Also arrested were lesser known guys Nicholas Ferriola, Joseph Venezia, Thomas Johnson, Dennis Johnson, and Michael Ricci.

One named defendant had been found deceased in a hotel room and three notorious killers—Nicholas W. Calabrese, Frank Calabrese, Sr., and Paul Schiro—were already in federal custody.

I was stunned! I never thought the feds would be able to break the Outfit open like they were cracking an egg, but the way I interpreted the release, they had. Although the release didn't provide the specific details of any of the murders, it was understandable that the government didn't want to present its evidence until the trial. Even so, I had the feeling they had put together a powerful case. However, it would be another two years before the deaths of Tony and Michael were discussed in open court by one of their killers.

* * *

In June 2007, the Family Secrets trial got underway in Chicago. On July 19, the big news out of the courtroom was the testimony of Nick Calabrese about the murders of Tony and Michael Spilotro. When I read it, my fucking blood started boiling. The cause of my anger wasn't that they were killed but the method the killers used.

They weren't beaten to death in a cornfield as depicted in *Casino* but in the basement of a house in a Chicago suburb where Calabrese and ten or so other mobsters were waiting. Calabrese said Michael Spilotro came down the stairs first. Calabrese said hello to Michael and then tackled him around the legs, bringing him down. He said that as Michael was falling, one of the other hitters, Louie the Mooch Eboli, wrapped a rope around Michael's neck.

Tony must have quickly realized that he had walked into a trap he wasn't going to get out of. Calabrese said that while he was subduing Michael he said he heard Tony say only one thing, "Can I say a prayer?"

I believe that Calabrese told it straight because Tony would never beg for anything—not even his life.

Calabrese continued that after Tony was wrestled to the floor joining Michael, the beatings began in earnest. Using fists and feet, the killers rained blows on the brothers until they were dead. Their bodies were taken to a cornfield in Indiana and buried in a shallow grave.

The government's case was strong, and the four killers

who were still alive were all convicted. Joey Lombardo, Frank Calabrese, and James Marcello each received life sentences. Because of his cooperation, Nick Calabrese got only twelve years. As I mulled things over I couldn't get my mind off Louie Eboli. I had asked Tony for permission to kill Louie years earlier, and he turned me down. Maybe in those last few seconds of his life as he watched Louie put the rope around his brother's neck, he wished he'd have given me the okay. It wouldn't have made any difference, though. If Louie hadn't done it somebody else would have. Tony and Michael were doomed when they agreed to go to that meeting. Nothing could have saved them.

AFTERWORD

In closing, I want to recap what I've told you and account for some of the people I've talked about. I hope I made it clear that Tony Spilotro was a tough guy, a thief, a gambler, and a killer—all of which are assets to someone wanting to become a successful gangster. He had a sense of humor and wasn't above playing practical jokes. He made a lot of money for the Outfit and himself and functioned as kind of a trouble shooter for them by eliminating several problems. You can find various published articles stating that Tony was suspected of up to twenty-four murders. I place his body count at fifteen, but admit there may have been more. The actual total will probably never be known.

However, Tony was also very ambitious and power hungry—traits that can get you into trouble when living "the life." The other major thing that worked against him was his inability to control his sex drive. Most of his affairs only caused him marital problems, but I believe his dalliance with Geri Rosenthal was a contributing factor in the Outfit's decision to kill him.

What was the aftermath of the Outfit's ouster from Las Vegas? Did all organized crime disappear from Sin City? No, but their activities are entirely different now—they aren't running the casinos, corporations are. I believe they might be involved in the adult entertainment business and there are bookies and drug dealers, too, but it isn't organized like it used to be. Those days are gone. I still see some Outfit-connected guys in Vegas. A few of them live there, but mostly they're on vacation.

The face of crime in Vegas may have changed, but there is still crime—lots of it. What they have now are the street gangs, and the gangsters of my day pale in comparison to them when it comes to violence. They kill the innocent without hesitation and for no real reason.

When people ask me if Vegas was better when the Mob ran it, my answer is that for civilians, it was a hell of a lot safer.

Now, let's see what happened to some of the other players.

Joey Hansen

Joey died of cancer prior to the 2005 indictments in the FBI's Operation Family Secrets investigation. The feds had DNA evidence tying him to the Emil Vaci murder, and he would have been indicted had the Grim Reaper not gotten him first.

Dicky Gorman

I believe it was in 1966 that Dicky suffered a nervous breakdown and was locked up in a hospital psych ward for a week. When they let him out he was placed on heavy-duty medication and told to keep away from alcohol while using it. One night his wife went out, and when she left he was on the couch watching TV. When she returned home he was still on the couch and appeared to have fallen asleep.

However, when she attempted to wake him the next morning she found he wasn't asleep—he was dead. There were two empty beer cans on the floor near the couch. Apparently he died from a reaction to mixing alcohol with the drugs he was taking.

Paulie Schiro

Paulie was convicted of racketeering in the Family Secrets trial and sentenced to twenty years in federal prison.

Hole in the Wall Gang

Ernie Davino, Leo Guardino, and Wayne Matecki are all still alive and free as far as I know.

Joe Blasko

The former-cop-turned-crook passed away from natural causes in November 2002 at his home in Utah. He was sixty-seven.

Lefty Rosenthal
Following the car bombing Lefty relocated to Florida, where he ran a successful sports betting website and served as a consultant to offshore sports wagering companies. He died of natural causes on October 13, 2008.

Geri Rosenthal
After splitting with Lefty, Geri moved to Los Angeles where she was found unconscious in a Sunset Boulevard motel on November 6, 1982. She died in the hospital three days later, and her death was ruled an accidental drug overdose.

Sal Romano
As far as I know, Sal is still in the Witness Protection Program. The last I heard his health was failing and he was in a wheelchair, but he was still alive.

Oscar Goodman
Oscar continued practicing law until he was elected mayor of Las Vegas in 1999. He was reelected in 2003 and 2007 but was term-limited from running again. He also appeared as himself in *Casino*.

Personally, I never cared for Oscar and thought there were several lawyers in Vegas better than him. Tony really liked him, though, and paid him a lot of money over the years. I remember one day I was riding with Tony when he stopped at Oscar's office. When we pulled up Tony said, "See that building, Frankie? I paid for it."

Nancy & Vincent Spilotro
After Tony was killed I didn't hear a lot about Nancy or

Vincent. I learned that Nancy had remained in Las Vegas and heard Vincent was going back and forth between Vegas and Los Angeles where he was receiving treatment for some type of medical condition. I later read that both of them had some involvement with the now-defunct Mob Attraction (originally the Mob Experience) at the Tropicana and that Vincent was making a few dollars selling family photos and other memorabilia on the Internet. Other than that, I didn't know how things were going for them.

That changed on August 28, 2013, when I was in line at a pharmacy in Las Vegas talking to the clerk at the counter. The place was busy, and several people were sitting around waiting to pick up their medications. I said something to the clerk, and then this female voice from behind me said, "Is that right, Frankie?"

I turned around, but wasn't sure who had spoken. I just said, "My name ain't Frankie."

An older lady I didn't recognize said, "Oh yes it is. I'd know your voice, anywhere."

As she got out of her chair and started walking toward me I still didn't know who she was. And then she said, "It's me, Nancy." Only then did I realize it was Nancy Spilotro, Tony's widow. I hadn't seen her since I testified against Tony at the M&M Murders trial in Chicago in 1983.

I stood there expecting a slap across my face when she got to me. But, instead, she hugged me and kissed me on the cheek. She said, "Tony and I never hated you, Frank. Even after you rolled, we never hated you."

Nancy and I talked there in the store for almost an hour—it was very emotional for me. I'm not going to go into detail, but life hadn't been very kind to her following Tony's murder. I figured he'd left her in pretty good shape financially, but apparently he either hadn't or the money had all been spent. She told me she was having trouble paying for her medicines and basic living costs. I felt bad for her and gave her $300 to help with some of her expenses.

I asked her if she ever heard from Oscar Goodman or anybody else from the old days. She said nobody had anything to do with her after Tony's murder. Considering all the money Tony paid Oscar over the years, I think he could have done better by her.

As for Vincent, Nancy said he was having major ongoing health problems. In fact, in early 2016 a source in Chicago told me that the word on the streets was that Vincent had died. I learned later that forty-nine-year-old Vincent Spilotro died in Vegas on November 28, 2015, of a drug overdose. I'm confident the rumors were true and that was Tony's son.

Anyway, when we parted, I was relieved that Nancy hadn't held a grudge against me all those years, as I'd thought she had.

I'm sorry she lost her husband and son and that her life has taken other bad turns. But, in reality, very few Mob stories have happy endings.

Use this link to sign up for advance notice
of Frank Cullotta's and Dennis N. Griffin's Next Book:
http://wildbluepress.com/AdvanceNotice

Word-of-mouth is critical to an author's long-term success.

If you appreciated this book please leave a review on the
Amazon sales page:
http://wbp.bz/mobstera

WILDBLUE
P R E S S

Available Now From WildBlue Press:
BETRAYAL IN BLUE by BURL BARER,
FRANK C. GIRARDOT JR., and KEN EURELL

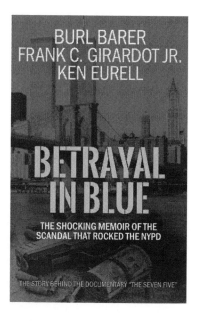

BURL BARER
FRANK C. GIRARDOT JR.
KEN EURELL

BETRAYAL
IN BLUE

THE SHOCKING MEMOIR OF THE
SCANDAL THAT ROCKED THE NYPD

THE STORY BEHIND THE DOCUMENTARY "THE SEVEN FIVE"

They Had No Fear Of The Cops
Because They Were The Cops

NYPD officers Mike Dowd and Kenny Eurell knew there
were two ways to get rich quick in Brooklyn's Lower East
Side. You either became drug dealers, or you robbed drug
dealers. They decided to do both.

Read More: **http://wbp.bz/bib**

Available Now From WildBlue Press:
REPEAT OFFENDER by Bradley Nickell

"Best True Crime Book of 2015" (Suspense Magazine) A "Sin City" cop recounts his efforts to catch one of the most prolific criminals to ever walk the neon-lit streets of Las Vegas. "If you like mayhem, madness, and suspense, Repeat Offender is the book to read."(Aphrodite Jones, New York Times bestselling author)

Read More: **http://wbp.bz/ro**

 WILDBLUE PRESS

See even more at:
http://wbp.bz/tc

More True Crime You'll Love From WildBlue Press

RAW DEAL by Gil Valle

RAW DEAL: The Untold Story of the NYPD's "Cannibal Cop" is the memoir of Gil Valle, written with co-author Brian Whitney. It is part the controversial saga of a man who was imprisoned for "thought crimes," and a look into an online world of dark sexuality and violence that most people don't know exists, except maybe in their nightmares.

wbp.bz/rawdeal

BETRAYAL IN BLUE by Burl Barer & Frank C. Girardot Jr.

Adapted from Ken Eurell's shocking personal memoir, plus hundreds of hours of exclusive interviews with the major players, including former international drug lord, Adam Diaz, and Dori Eurell, revealing the truth behind what you won't see in the hit documentary THE SEVEN FIVE.

wbp.bz/bib

THE POLITICS OF MURDER by Margo Nash

"A chilling story about corruption, political power and a stacked judicial system in Massachusetts."–John Ferak, bestselling author of FAILURE OF JUSTICE.

wbp.bz/pom

FAILURE OF JUSTICE by John Ferak

If the dubious efforts of law enforcement that led to the case behind MAKING A MURDERER made you cringe, your skin will crawl at the injustice portrayed in FAILURE OF JUSTICE: A Brutal Murder, An Obsessed Cop, Six Wrongful Convictions. Award-winning journalist and bestselling author John Ferak pursued the story of the Beatrice 6 who were wrongfully accused of the brutal, ritualistic rape and murder of an elderly widow in Beatrice, Nebraska, and then railroaded by law enforcement into prison for a crime they did not commit.

wbp.bz/foj

Made in the
USA
Middletown, DE